Determination of Total Organic Carbon and Specific UV Absorbance at 254 nm in Source Water and Drinking Water

U.S. Environmental Protection Agency

The BiblioGov Project is an effort to expand awareness of the public documents and records of the U.S. Government via print publications. In broadening the public understanding of government and its work, an enlightened democracy can grow and prosper. Ranging from historic Congressional Bills to the most recent Budget of the United States Government, the BiblioGov Project spans a wealth of government information. These works are now made available through an environmentally friendly, print-on-demand basis, using only what is necessary to meet the required demands of an interested public. We invite you to learn of the records of the U.S. Government, heightening the knowledge and debate that can lead from such publications.

Included are the following Collections:

Budget of The United States Government	Code of Federal Regulations
Presidential Documents	Congressional Documents
United States Code	Economic Indicators
Education Reports from ERIC	Federal Register
GAO Reports	Government Manuals
History of Bills	House Journal
House Rules and Manual	Privacy act Issuances
Public and Private Laws	Statutes at Large

EPA Document #: EPA/600/R-09/122

METHOD 415.3 **DETERMINATION OF TOTAL ORGANIC CARBON AND SPECIFIC UV ABSORBANCE AT 254 nm IN SOURCE WATER AND DRINKING WATER**

Revision 1.2
September, 2009

B. B. Potter, USEPA, Office of Research and Development, National Exposure Research Laboratory
J. C. Wimsatt, The National Council On The Aging, Senior Environmental Employment Program

NATIONAL EXPOSURE RESEARCH LABORATORY
OFFICE OF RESEARCH AND DEVELOPMENT
U.S. ENVIRONMENTAL PROTECTION AGENCY
CINCINNATI, OHIO 45268

METHOD 415.3
DETERMINATION OF TOTAL ORGANIC CARBON AND SPECIFIC UV ABSORBANCE AT 254 nm IN SOURCE WATER AND DRINKING WATER

1.0 SCOPE AND APPLICATION

1.1 This method provides procedures for the determination of total organic carbon (TOC), dissolved organic carbon (DOC), and UV absorption at 254 nm (UVA) in source waters and drinking waters. The DOC and UVA determinations are used in the calculation of the Specific UV Absorbance (SUVA). For TOC and DOC analysis, the sample is acidified and the inorganic carbon (IC) is removed prior to analysis for organic carbon (OC) content using a TOC instrument system. The measurements of TOC and DOC are based on calibration with potassium hydrogen phthalate (KHP) standards. This method is not intended for use in the analysis of treated or untreated industrial wastewater discharges as those wastewater samples may damage or contaminate the instrument system(s).

1.2 The three (3) day, pooled organic carbon detection limit (OCDL) is based on the detection limit (DL) calculation.[1] It is a statistical determination of precision, and may be below the level of quantitation. The determination of OCDL is dependent on the analytical instrument system's precision, the purity of laboratory reagent water (LRW), and the skill of the analyst. Different TOC instrument systems have produced significantly different OCDLs that range between 0.02 and 0.12 mg/L OC for both TOC and DOC measurements. Examples of these data can be seen in Section 17, Table 17.1. It should be noted that background levels of OC contamination are problematic. The minimum reporting level (MRL) for TOC and DOC will depend on the laboratory's ability to control background levels (Sect. 4).

2.0 SUMMARY OF METHOD

2.1 In both TOC and DOC determinations, organic carbon in the water sample is oxidized to produce carbon dioxide (CO_2), which is then measured by a detection system. There are two different approaches for the oxidation of organic carbon in water samples to carbon dioxide gas: (a) combustion in an oxidizing gas and (b) UV promoted or heat catalyzed chemical oxidation with a persulfate solution. Carbon dioxide, which is released from the oxidized sample, is detected by a conductivity detector or by a nondispersive infrared (NDIR) detector. Instruments using any combination of the above technologies may be used in this method.

2.2 Settleable solids and floating matter may cause plugging of valves, tubing, and the injection needle and/or injection port. The TOC procedure allows the removal of settleable solids and floating matter. The suspended matter is considered part of the sample. The resulting water sample is then considered a close approximation of the original whole water sample for the purpose of TOC measurement.

2.3 The DOC procedure requires that the sample be passed through a 0.45-μm filter prior to analysis to remove particulate OC from the sample.

2.4 The TOC and DOC procedures require that all IC be removed from the sample before the sample is analyzed for organic carbon content. If the IC is not completely removed, **significant error will occur.** The sample, which is then free from IC interference, is injected into a TOC instrument system. The organic carbon is oxidized to CO_2, which is released from the sample, detected, and reported as mg/L or ppm TOC or DOC.

2.5 The UVA procedure requires that the sample be passed through a 0.45-μm filter and transferred to a quartz cell. It is then placed in a spectrophotometer to measure the UV absorbance at 254 nm and reported in cm^{-1}.

2.6 The SUVA calculation requires both the DOC and UVA measurement. The SUVA is calculated by dividing the UV absorbance of the sample (in cm^{-1}) by the DOC of the sample (in mg/L) and then multiplying by 100 cm/M. SUVA is reported in units of L/mg-M. The formula for the SUVA may be found in Section 12.2.

3.0 DEFINITIONS AND TERMS
NOTE: *To assist the reader, a table of acronyms can be found in Section 3.20.*

3.1 ANALYSIS BATCH - A set of samples prepared and analyzed on the same instrument during a 24-hour period. For a TOC/DOC analysis batch, the set may contain: calibration standards, laboratory reagent blank and/or filter blanks, field blank, field samples, laboratory fortified matrix sample, field duplicate sample, and continuing calibration check standards. For a UVA analysis batch, the set may contain: filter blanks, field samples, field blank, field duplicate sample, and spectrophotometer check solutions with associated blank. An analysis batch is limited to 20 field samples. QC samples are not counted towards the 20 sample limit. QC requirements are summarized in Table 17.6.

3.2 BLANKS - Prepared from a volume of LRW (Sect. 3.9) and used as needed to fulfill quality assurance requirements and to monitor the analytical system.

3.2.1 CALIBRATION BLANK (CB) - The calibration blank is a volume of LRW that is treated with the same reagents used in the preparation of the calibration standards. The CB is a "zero standard" and is used to calibrate the TOC instrument. The CB is made at the same time as the calibration standards and stored along with and under the same conditions as the calibration standards. The CB is also used to monitor increases in organic background found in the calibration standards over time by analyzing it as a sample and comparing the results with initial analysis of the CB.

- 3.2.2 FIELD REAGENT BLANK (FRB) - A volume, equivalent to that which is collected at a sample site, of LRW is placed in a sample bottle or vial. A second empty sample bottle or vial accompanies the LRW sample container to the sample site. At the sample site, the LRW is transferred into the empty bottle or vial which then becomes the FRB. The FRB is treated as a sample in all respects including shipment from the sampling site, exposure to the sampling site conditions, storage, preservation, and all analytical procedures. The purpose of the FRB is to determine if the TOC, DOC, and UVA measurements of the samples collected in the field are free from interferences or contamination as a result of the sample collection procedure and/or transport of the sample(s) to the laboratory. The FRB is optional and is usually used when the laboratory suspects a problem in sample collection and handling.

- 3.2.3 FILTER BLANK (FB) - The FB is an aliquot of LRW that is filtered and analyzed using the same procedures as field samples undergoing DOC and UVA determinations. For DOC and UVA analyses, the FB serves as the LRB. The FB will give an indication of overall contribution of organic carbon contamination from laboratory sources such as the LRW itself, labware cleaning procedures, reagents, the filter apparatus, filter, and instrument system(s).

- 3.2.4 LABORATORY REAGENT BLANK (LRB) - A volume of LRW that is prepared with each sample set and is treated exactly as a TOC sample including exposure to all glassware, plasticware, equipment, and reagents that are used with other samples. The LRB is used to determine if organic contamination or other interferences are present in the laboratory environment, reagents, apparatus, or procedures. The LRB must be acidified and sparged following the same procedure as is used to prepare the TOC sample(s).

3.3 CALIBRATION SOLUTIONS - Calibration should be performed according to the manufacturer's operation manual. The following solutions are used to calibrate the TOC instrument system for TOC or DOC determinations (calibration solutions are not used for UVA determination):

- 3.3.1 ORGANIC CARBON PRIMARY DILUTION STANDARD (OC-PDS) - A concentrated solution containing potassium hydrogen phthalate (KHP) in LRW water that is prepared in the laboratory or is an assayed KHP standard solution purchased from a commercial source. The OC-PDS is used for the preparation of organic carbon calibration standards (OC-CAL), continuing calibration check standards (CCC), and laboratory fortified matrix samples (LFM).

    3.3.2 ORGANIC CARBON CALIBRATION STANDARD (OC-CAL) - A solution prepared from the OC-PDS and diluted with LRW to various concentrations. The OC-CAL solutions are used to calibrate the instrument response with respect to organic carbon concentration.

    3.3.3 CONTINUING CALIBRATION CHECK (CCC) - An OC-CAL solution which is analyzed periodically to verify the accuracy of the existing calibration of the instrument (Sect. 10.3).

3.4 DISSOLVED ORGANIC CARBON (DOC) - Organic matter, contained in a water sample that is soluble and/or colloidal, that can pass through a 0.45-µm filter.

3.5 FIELD DUPLICATES (FD1 and FD2) - Two separate samples collected at the same time and place under identical circumstances, and treated exactly the same throughout field and laboratory procedures. Analyses of FD1 and FD2 give a measure of the precision associated with sample collection, preservation, and storage, as well as laboratory procedures.

3.6 INORGANIC CARBON (IC) - Carbon in water samples from non organic sources, composed mainly from dissolved mineral carbonates and carbon dioxide. IC can interfere with the determination of TOC and DOC if it is not removed.

3.7 LABORATORY FORTIFIED BLANK (LFB) – An aliquot of LRW or other blank matrix to which a known quantity of KHP is added in the laboratory. The LFB is subjected to the same preparation and analysis as a sample. The purpose of the LFB is to determine whether the methodology is in control, and whether the laboratory is capable of making accurate and precise measurements. For this method, a TOC LFB is the same as a CCC (Sect. 10.3) and no additional LFB is required. One LFB is required with each DOC analysis batch. No LFB is required for UVA analysis.

3.8 LABORATORY FORTIFIED SAMPLE MATRIX (LFM) - An aliquot of a field sample to which a known quantity of KHP is added in the laboratory. The LFM is subjected to the same preparation and analysis as a sample, and its purpose is to determine whether the sample matrix affects the accuracy of the TOC or DOC analytical results. The background concentration of organic carbon in the sample matrix must be determined in a separate aliquot and the measured value in the LFM corrected for background concentration.

3.9 LABORATORY REAGENT WATER (LRW) - The LRW may be distilled and/or deionized (DI) water, or high pressure liquid chromatography (HPLC) reagent grade or equivalent water which is low in TOC concentration, meeting the requirements as stated in Section 7.2.

3.10 MATERIAL SAFETY DATA SHEET (MSDS) - Written information provided by a vendor describing a chemical's toxicity, health hazards, physical and chemical properties (flammability, reactivity, etc.), storage, handling, and spill precautions.

3.11 MINIMUM REPORTING LEVEL (MRL) - The minimum concentration of organic carbon that can be reported as a quantified value in a sample following analysis. This concentration is determined by the background level of the analyte in the LRBs and the sensitivity of the method to organic carbon. See Section 9.10 for guidelines in the establishment of the MRL.

3.12 ORGANIC CARBON DETECTION LIMIT (OCDL) - The calculated minimum concentration of a known amount of organic carbon (OC) added to the LRW that can be identified, measured as either TOC or DOC, and reported with 99% confidence that the OC concentration is greater than zero as per the procedure in Section 9.2.7.

3.13 ORGANIC CARBON (OC) - In this method, when a concentration or instrument reading applies to either a TOC or DOC determination, the term "OC" may be used. For example, the LRB must not exceed 0.35 mg/L OC.

3.14 ORGANIC MATTER - A mixture of organic compounds (carbon-carbon, carbon-hydrogen bonded compounds) naturally occurring and/or man-made that are found in source water used by drinking water utilities. The quantity and quality of the OM in source water is measured by TOC/DOC instrument systems or is measured by UVA.

3.15 QUALITY CONTROL SAMPLE (QCS) - A solution containing a known concentration of an organic carbon compound(s) which is analyzed exactly like a sample. The QCS is obtained from a source external to the laboratory and is different from the source used for preparing the calibration standards. It is used to check laboratory and instrument performance.

3.16 SOURCE WATER - Surface water or ground water that is used by a drinking water utility to produce potable water for public consumption.

3.17 SPECIFIC UV ABSORBANCE AT 254 nm (SUVA) - A measure of DOC aromatic content that is calculated by measuring the DOC and the UV absorbance at 254 nm of a 0.45-μm filtered water sample. SUVA is calculated according to the equation given in Section 12.2.

3.18 TOTAL CARBON (TC) - A measure of the OC and IC contained in a water sample. In this method, IC is removed from the sample. Therefore, the TC reported by a TOC instrument system will be equal to the TOC or DOC measurement.

3.19 TOTAL ORGANIC CARBON (TOC) - The gross amount of organic matter (carbon not removed by the IC removal step) found in natural water. Suspended particulate, colloidal, and dissolved organic matter are a part of the TOC measurement. For this method, the TOC definition excludes the contribution of floating vegetative or animal matter, and volatile organic matter found in source water. Settleable solids consisting of inorganic sediments and some organic particulate are not transferred from the sample by the laboratory analyst and are not a part of the TOC measurement.

3.20 TABLE OF ACRONYMS

Acronym	Term
CB	calibration blank
CCC	continuing calibration check
COMM-BKS	commercial spectrophotometer background solution
COMM-SCS	commercial spectrophotometer check solution
DOC	dissolved organic carbon
FB	filter blank
FD	field duplicate
FRB	field reagent blank
IC	inorganic carbon
IDC	initial demonstration of capability
KHP	potassium hydrogen phthalate
LFB	laboratory fortified blank
LFM	laboratory fortified matrix
LRB	laboratory reagent blank
LRW	laboratory reagent water
MRL	minimum reporting level
MSDS	material safety data sheet
OC-CAL	organic carbon calibration standard

Acronym	Term
OC-PDS	organic carbon primary dilution standard
OCDL	organic carbon detection limit
QCS	quality control sample
SCS	spectrophotometer check solution
SDWA	Safe Drinking Water Act
SOP	standard operating procedure
SUVA	specific UV absorbance
TC	total carbon
TOC	total organic carbon
UVA	UV absorbance

4.0 CONTAMINATION AND INTERFERENCES

4.1 SPECIAL CONSIDERATIONS FOR ONSITE UTILITY LABORATORIES - Aerosols (foam and mist) from the operation of a water treatment plant contain organic carbon and will contaminate glassware, reagents, sample collection equipment, and onsite laboratory equipment if they are exposed to air at the water utility. For an onsite laboratory, it is recommended that air be filtered and isolated from organic fumes generated by petroleum products and combustion gases which come from the operation of some water utility equipment. Work traffic in the onsite laboratory should be minimized as it may produce dust containing organic matter that will result in the contamination of unprotected samples and laboratory equipment.

4.2 All glassware must be meticulously cleaned. Wash glassware with detergent and tap water, rinse with tap water followed by reagent water. Non-volumetric glassware may then be heated in a muffle furnace at 425 °C for 2 hours to eliminate interferences. Volumetric glassware should not be heated above 120 °C. Alternate cleaning procedures, such as acid rinsing and heating at lower temperatures, may be employed, providing that these procedures are documented in a laboratory SOP and LRBs are monitored as per Section 9.9.

4.3 Laboratory water systems have been known to contaminate samples due to bacterial breakthrough from resin beds, activated carbon, and filters. Laboratory water systems should be maintained and monitored frequently for carbon background and bacterial growth. It is recommended that the LRW be filtered through a 0.22-μm filter membrane to prevent bacterial contamination of TOC instrument systems, reagents, and samples. The LRW, sample transfer (pipet), glassware, and sample bottles are the principle source for organic background in the analytical system. However, it is not possible to control all sources of organic carbon contamination. Therefore, this method allows for instrument background correction or adjusting the zero reference point of the instrument for organic carbon background that is found in the analytical system.[2] There are many ways to correct for organic carbon background. Consult the instrument manufacturer's operation manual for the instrument background correction procedure. **Subtraction of LRB or FB measurements from TOC, DOC, or UVA sample results is not allowed.**

4.4 High concentrations of OC, both man-made and naturally occurring, can cause gross contamination of the instrument system, changes in calibration, and damage to valves, pumps, tubing, and other components. It is recommended that analysis of a sample known to have a concentration of OC > 10 mg/L OC be followed by the analysis of an LRB. It is highly recommended that known samples containing OC concentrations > 50 mg/L OC be diluted or not run on instruments used to analyze low-level drinking water samples.

4.5 Source waters containing ionic iron, nitrates, nitrites, and bromide have been reported to interfere with measurements of UVA absorbance at 254 nm.[3] The concentration of the interferences and their effect on the UVA cannot be determined as each unique sample matrix may produce a different UVA response for the same concentration of interference or combination of interferences. This method does not treat or remove these interferences. Therefore, suspected or known interferences may affect results and must be flagged in the SUVA result as "suspected UVA interferences."

4.6 Chloride exceeding 250 mg/L may interfere with persulfate oxidation methods.[4,5] Some instrument systems may require increased persulfate concentration and extended oxidation times. Consult with your instrument manufacturer's representative or instrument operation manual for instrument settings and reagent strengths when analyzing samples containing high levels of chloride.

4.7 Inorganic carbon (IC) interferes with TOC and DOC measurements. TOC instrument bias due to incomplete IC removal has been reported.[6,7] If inorganic carbon is not completely removed from the water sample, it will result in a positive or negative bias depending on the way the instrument system calculates TOC (e.g., TOC = TC - IC, TC = TOC + IC, or TOC = TC). When inorganic carbon (IC) is removed from the sample prior to the TOC assay, as required in this method, TOC = TC and the method bias is minimized.

5.0 SAFETY

5.1 Fast-moving source water, steep inclines, water conduits, and electrical hazards may present special safety considerations for the sample collector. The sample collector should be aware of any potential safety hazards and take necessary precautions while collecting samples.

5.2 Each chemical reagent used in this method should be regarded as a potential health hazard. Exposure to these compounds should be minimized and/or avoided by active participation in safety planning and good laboratory practices.[8] Each laboratory is responsible for maintaining a current awareness file of OSHA regulations[9] regarding the safe handling of the chemicals specified in this method. Material Safety Data Sheets (MSDS) containing information on chemical and physical hazards associated with each chemical should be made available to all personnel involved in the chemical analysis.

5.3 Potassium persulfate is a strong oxidizing and corrosive reagent. The analyst should avoid eye and skin contact by wearing eye/face protection, powderless gloves and laboratory clothing. If body tissue comes in contact with this reagent, apply large quantities of water for at least 15 minutes (see MSDS) while removing contaminated clothing. This reagent may cause delayed burns. Seek immediate medical attention if the area becomes irritated or burned. This reagent can also cause a fire or explosion if it is allowed to come in contact with combustible materials.

5.4 Protect your hands by wearing laboratory disposable gloves during the preparation and disposal of corrosive (acids and oxidants) laboratory reagents. Do not reuse laboratory gloves that have been discarded or are suspected of being contaminated.

6.0 EQUIPMENT AND SUPPLIES

NOTE: *Brand names, and/or catalog numbers are included for illustrative purposes only. No endorsement is implied. Equivalent performance may be achieved using apparatus, instrument systems, and reagents other than those that are illustrated below. The laboratory is responsible for the assurance that alternate products, apparatus, instrument systems, and reagents demonstrate equivalent performance as specified in this method.*

6.1 FILTER APPARATUS - Nalgene® or Corning® 250 mL Filter System, 0.45-µm Nylon (NYL) or Polyethersulfone (PES) Low Extractable Membrane/Polystyrene Body with optional glass fiber prefilters (nominal 1 to 7 um). Packaging and filter apparatus are recyclable (NALGE-NUNC International: Nalgene Labware CAT. numbers NYL: 153-0045, PES: 168-0045). It is recommended that filter membranes be hydrophilic 0.45-µm filter material.

NOTE: *Alternate filter membranes (e.g., polypropylene, silver or Teflon®), apparatus technologies such as cartridges, reusable filter bodies, syringe filters, and their associated syringes, peristaltic pumps or vacuum pumps may be selected. The complexity of an alternative filter apparatus is left to the analyst's ingenuity providing that the apparatus meets quality control and initial demonstration of* *capability requirements as stated in Section 9.3.2, and that FB requirements are met (Sect. 9.9). It is recommended that the analyst review the AWWA journal article "Selecting filter membranes for measuring DOC and UV_{254}", Karanfil, et. al.[10], prior to the selection of an alternative filter membrane, apparatus, and wash procedure. Karanfil tested 11 filter membranes (0.45-µm pore size and 47-mm disc size) representing four different manufacturers and seven different types of filter materials for both desorption and adsorption. Hydrophilic polyethersulfone (PES) filters available from two manufacturers (Osmonics Micro-PES and Gelman Supor 450, both 0.45 micron absolute pore size and 47-mm disc size) and a hydrophilic polypropylene filter (Gelman GH Polypro, 0.45 micron absolute pore size and 47-mm disc size) were found to be the best options among those tested in the study.*

6.2 INJECTION VIALS - Specially cleaned 40-mL glass vials, with caps and polytetrafluoroethylene (PTFE)/silicone septa. Eagle-Picher TOC Certified, Cat. No. 40C-TOC/LL, Eagle-Picher Technologies®. These vials are specially cleaned by the manufacturing process and certified to contain < 10 µg TOC. Vials may be reused if cleaned as per Section 4.2. The PTFE/silicone septa once pierced by the sample injector must be discarded.

6.3 INSTRUMENT SYSTEMS - The TOC and UVA procedures allow for the use of several different types or combinations of TOC instrumental system technologies. Examples of typical TOC instrument systems, as well as a UV spectrophotometer, are described below. Data from these instruments may be found in Section 17. Only one TOC instrument is required to perform this method.

    6.3.1 TOC INSTRUMENT 1: UV/Persulfate/Wet Oxidation with Permeation/Conductivity Detection. The Ionics-Sievers® 800 TOC analyzer is based on UV catalyzed persulfate digestion to produce CO_2, which is detected by a membrane permeation/conductivity detector.

    6.3.2 TOC INSTRUMENT 2: Elevated Temperature/Catalyzed/Persulfate/Wet Oxidation/Nondispersive Infrared Detection (NDIR). The O.I. Analytical® TOC Model 1010 is based on elevated temperature (95-100°C) catalyzed persulfate digestion to produce CO_2, which is then detected by an NDIR detector.

    6.3.3 TOC INSTRUMENT 3: UV/Low Temperature/Persulfate/Wet Oxidation/NDIR. The Tekmar-Dohrmann® Phoenix 8000 TOC analyzer is based on UV catalyzed persulfate digestion to produce CO_2, which is then detected by an NDIR detector.

    6.3.4 TOC INSTRUMENT 4: Catalyzed/Combustion Oxidation(680 °C)/NDIR. The Shimadzu® model TOC-5000A analyzer is based on a catalyzed combustion in air or oxygen reagent gas to produce CO_2, which is then detected by an NDIR detector.

6.3.5 TOC INSTRUMENT 5: High Temperature Combustion Oxidation/NDIR. The Thermo Environmental® ThermoGlas™ 1200 TOC is based on a dual zone furnace with individually adjustable ovens from 700 to 1250 °C for final high temperature combustion of the sample with air or oxygen reagent gas to produce CO_2, which is then detected by an NDIR detector.

6.3.6 UV SPECTROPHOTOMETER: The spectrophotometer is used for the UVA determination only. The spectrophotometer must be able to measure UVA (254 nm), with an absorbance from 0.0045 to at least 1.0 cm^{-1} UVA, and accommodates a sample cell with a path length of 1, 5, or 10 cm.

6.4 LABORATORY REAGENT WATER TREATMENT SYSTEM - The LRW used for the development of this method was generated using a Millipore®, Milli-Q Plus Ultra-Pure Water Treatment System with a 0.22-μm sterile pack filter capable of producing organic carbon free (< 0.010 mg/L OC), ultrapure deionized water.[11] The maximum amount of OC allowed in the LRW for this method is 0.35 mg/L. When purchasing a treatment system for general laboratory use, it is recommended that a system be purchased capable of producing LRW of the above stated quality in order to be of use in other laboratory analyses.

6.5 MUFFLE FURNACE - A muffle furnace capable of heating up to 425 °C.

6.6 FIELD SAMPLE pH TEST - Sample pH indicator test strips, non-bleeding (colorpHast® Indicator Strips 0 - 2.5, cat. 9580), EM Science, 480 Democrat Road, Gibbstown, N.J. 08027. Pocket pH test kits, pocket pH meters, or laboratory pH meters are acceptable for field sample pH measurements.

6.7 PIPET, DISPOSABLE TRANSFER - Large volume bulb (15mL), non-sterile, with flexible long stem polyethylene transfer pipet. "Sedi-Pet ™", Fisher Scientific® Cat. 13-711-36. Pipets are used for sample transfer from the middle of a sample bottle containing floating material (scum).

6.8 SAMPLE COLLECTION REAGENT BOTTLES - Specially cleaned, 1-L Boston round glass bottles with cap. Eagle-Picher TOC Certified, Cat. No. 112-01A/C TOC, Eagle-Picher Technologies, LLC. These bottles are specially cleaned by the manufacturing process and certified to meet EPA OSWER Directive # 9240.0-05A "Specifications And Guidance For Contaminant-Free Sample Containers 12/92." Amber bottles are preferred, but clear glass bottles may be used if care is taken to protect samples from light. The laboratory may select glass bottles of any volume that meet the utility and laboratory sample processing and quality control sampling needs.

Glass bottles may be reused after cleaning (see Sect. 4.2 for glassware cleaning instructions) or discarded.

6.9 SPARGE APPARATUS - N-EVAP™, Nitrogen Evaporator System Model 111, Organomation Associates Inc. This apparatus is not used for its originally designed purpose of evaporating sample extracts. In this method, the apparatus is used as a sparging device. The stainless steel needles of the apparatus are lowered into the 40-mL sample vials containing the TOC or DOC samples to remove inorganic carbon by sparging with nitrogen gas.

Alternately, some TOC auto-samplers provide a pre-sparging or membrane IC removal option prior to injection of the sample into the TOC instrument system. The analyst is encouraged to utilize these instrument options, if available. Another alternative is for the laboratory analyst to fabricate a sparging apparatus. For example, an apparatus may consist of copper tubing from a regulated gas source, connected to a needle valve used for gas flow control, a length of silicone tubing with a glass Pasteur pipet inserted into the tubing and a ring stand with clamp for positioning the pipet. The Pasteur pipet is inserted into the sample bottle or vial to remove inorganic carbon by sparging with nitrogen gas (Sect. 11.5). The complexity of the alternative sparging apparatus is left to the analyst's ingenuity providing that the apparatus meets quality control and initial demonstration of capability (IC removal test) requirements as stated in Section 9.2.4.

6.10 VACUUM SOURCE - Aspirator, air flow or water flow, hand-operated or low pressure electric vacuum pump, providing a vacuum of 15 inches of mercury (Hg) or better. If an alternative choice is made, see note in Section 6.1.

6.11 VARIABLE PIPETTES - Programable automated pipettes. Rainin Instrument® EDP-Plus Pipette 10ml, Cat. No. EP-10 mL; EDP-Plus Pipette 1000 µL, Cat. No. EP-1000; EDP-Plus Pipette 100 µL, Cat. No. EP-100, or manual variable pipets with disposable tips having a calibrated range of 0 to 100-µL, 0 to 1000-µL, and 0 to 10 mL.

6.12 VOLUMETRIC FLASK AND PIPETS - All volumetric glassware used in this method are required to be "Class A".

6.13 WAVELENGTH VERIFICATION FILTER SET- Wavelength verification may be provided by the instrument manufacturer, a scientific instrument service company, or if this not practical, wavelength verification may be made by the laboratory using certified spectrophotometric filter sets with values traceable to NIST. Fisher Scientific Cat. No. 14-385-335, Spectronic No. 333150.

7.0 REAGENTS AND STANDARDS

NOTE: The chemicals required for this method must be at least reagent grade. Unless otherwise indicated, it is intended that all reagents shall conform to the specifications of the Committee on Analytical Reagents of the American Chemical Society (ACS) and/or ACS certified, when available. Some instrument manufacturers provide reagents specifically prepared for the optimum performance of their TOC instruments and provide calibration services and/or calibration standards. The analyst is allowed to use these services or prepare reagents and/or standards according to the instrument manufacturer's operation manual.

7.1 COMPRESSED GASES – Carbon dioxide free Ultra High Purity (UHP) grade nitrogen gas or an optional Ultra-low level TOC gas delivery system. For combustion based TOC systems, zero grade air and UHP grade oxygen may be needed. The use of lesser grades of compressed gases will result in high background noise in the TOC instrument systems. The TOC Instrument 1 described in Section 6.3.1. does not require compressed gasses for operation.

7.2 LABORATORY REAGENT WATER (LRW) - Water that has a TOC reading of ≤ 0.35 mg/L and ≤ 0.01 cm^{-1} UVA. Although the LRW TOC and UVA limits in this method are 0.35 mg/L and 0.01 cm^{-1}, respectively, the system specified in Section 6.4 is capable of producing better quality organic carbon free, ultrapure deionized water. For optimum performance, it is recommended that LRW with ≤ 0.05 mg/L TOC and ≤ 0.0045 cm^{-1} UVA be used for this method. Alternatively, LRW may be purchased (ACS HPLC grade or equivalent).

7.3 DISODIUM HYDROGEN PHOSPHATE, [Na_2HPO_4, CAS# 7558-79-4] - Anhydrous, ACS grade or better.

7.4 O-PHOSPHORIC ACID (85%), [H_3PO_4, CAS# 7664-38-2] - ACS grade or better.

7.5 POTASSIUM DIHYDROGEN PHOSPHATE, [KH_2PO_4, CAS# 7778-77-0]- Anhydrous, ACS grade or better.

7.6 POTASSIUM HYDROGEN PHTHALATE (KHP), [$C_8H_5O_4K$, CAS# 877-24-7] - Anhydrous, ACS grade or better.

7.7 REAGENT SOLUTIONS FOR WET CHEMICAL OXIDATION - It is assumed that each instrument manufacturer has optimized reagent solutions for their respective instruments and has provided the instructions for the preparation of reagents in the instrument's operation manual. NOTE: *TOC Instrument 1 does not require gas sparge of reagents as the manufacture provides reagent packs for the operation of the instrument.*

7.7.1 PERSULFATE REAGENT - Prepare this solution according to the instrument manufacturer's instructions or purchase the solution from the instrument manufacturer. If the laboratory prepares the solution, transfer the solution to the instrument reagent bottle and cap. It is recommended that this solution be sparged gently with carbon dioxide free UHP grade nitrogen gas for approximately 1 hour. If the instrument system provides continuous sparge, it is recommended that the reagent bottles be allowed to sparge for 10 minutes to 1 hour before operating the instrument. Self contained reagent packs or other types of reagent systems may not require reagent sparging. Discard the solution as per expiration time/date listed in the manufacturer's operation manual.

7.7.2 PHOSPHORIC ACID SOLUTION - Prepare this solution according to the instrument manufacturer's instructions or purchase the solution from the instrument manufacturer. If the laboratory prepares the solution, transfer the solution to the instrument reagent bottle and cap. It is recommended that this solution be sparged gently with carbon dioxide free UHP grade nitrogen gas for approximately 1 hour. If the instrument system provides continuous sparge, it is recommended that the reagent bottles be allowed to sparge for 10 minutes to 1 hour before operating the instrument. Self contained reagent packs or other types of reagent systems may not require reagent sparging. Discard the solution as per expiration time/date listed in the manufacturer's operation manual.

7.8 STANDARD SOLUTIONS
NOTE: *Consult with the instrument manufacturer or operation manual for the recommended concentrated acid used for preservation of standard solutions. The concentrated acid used to preserve the standards is usually HCl, H_2SO_4, or H_3PO_4 depending upon the instrument operation manual recommendation. The acid used for the standards must be the same as the one used for the samples. Standard solutions may be alternatively prepared in larger or smaller volumes and concentrations as needed for the calibration of instruments. Standard solutions may be prepared by gravimetric or volumetric techniques. This section provides guidance for the preparation of calibration solutions.*

7.8.1 INORGANIC CARBON PRIMARY TEST SOLUTION (IC-TEST) REAGENTS

7.8.1.1 AMMONIUM CHLORIDE, [NH_4Cl, CAS# 12125-02-9] - ACS grade or better.

7.8.1.2 CALCIUM CHLORIDE DIHYDRATE, [$CaCl_2 \cdot 2H_2O$, CAS# 10035-04-8] - ACS grade or better.

7.8.1.3 CALCIUM NITRATE TETRAHYDRATE, [$Ca(NO_3)_2 \cdot 4H_2O$, CAS# 13477-34-4] - ACS grade or better.

7.8.1.4 MAGNESIUM SULFATE HEPTAHYDRATE, [$MgSO_4 \cdot 7H_2O$, CAS# 10034-99-8] - ACS grade or better.

7.8.1.5 POTASSIUM CHLORIDE, [KCl, CAS# 7447-40-7] - ACS grade or better.

7.8.1.6 SODIUM BICARBONATE, [$NaHCO_3$, CAS# 144-55-8] - ACS grade or better.

7.8.1.7 SODIUM CHLORIDE, [$NaCl$, CAS# 7647-14-5] - ACS grade or better.

7.8.1.8 SODIUM-META SILICATE NONAHYDRATE, [$Na_2SiO_3 \cdot 9H_2O$, CAS# 13517-24-3]

7.8.1.9 SODIUM PHOSPHATE DIBASIC HEPTAHYDRATE, [$Na_2HPO_4 \cdot 7H_2O$, CAS# 7782-85-6] - ACS grade or better.

7.8.2 PREPARATION OF THE IC-TEST SOLUTION, 100 MG/L IC - This solution is used in the performance of the IC removal sparging efficiency test (Sect. 9.2.4). The ionic content of the IC-TEST mixture solution was chosen from a previous investigation in which the authors wanted to simulate waters likely to be found in waste treatment plants.[12] Because the inorganic salts are not soluble in a single concentrated solution, prepare four separate stock solutions by diluting each of the following to one liter with LRW:

FLASK (1 L)	SALT	WEIGHT (g)
A	magnesium sulfate heptahydrate, $MgSO_4 \cdot 7H_2O$	2.565
B	ammonium chloride, NH_4Cl	0.594
	calcium chloride dihydrate, $CaCl_2 \cdot 2H_2O$	2.050
	calcium nitrate tetrahydrate, $Ca(NO_3)_2 \cdot 4H_2O$	0.248
	potassium chloride, KCl	0.283
	sodium chloride, $NaCl$	0.281
C	sodium bicarbonate, $NaHCO_3$	2.806
	sodium phosphate dibasic heptahydrate, $Na_2HPO_4 \cdot 7H_2O$	0.705
D	sodium-meta silicate nonahydrate, $Na_2SiO_3 \cdot 9H_2O$	1.862

Prepare a 102.5 mg/L IC-TEST mixture, based on bicarbonate calculations and impurities, by adding a 10-mL aliquot of each of the above solutions to a 40-mL vial. Add 40 µL of H_3PO_4, HCl, or H_2SO_4, depending upon instrument requirements (see note, Sect. 7.8), to the 40-mL injection vial. An IC-TEST mixture of approximately 100 mg/L was chosen to represent the extreme inorganic carbon concentration the analyst may encounter. Although the mixture is turbid after preparation, clarification occurs after acidification.

7.8.3 ORGANIC CARBON PRIMARY DILUTION STANDARD (OC-PDS), 500 mg/L (1 mL = 0.5 mg OC) - Prepare an acid preserved (pH ≤2) OC-PDS by pouring approximately 500 mL of LRW into a 1-liter volumetric flask, adding 1 mL of concentrated acid for preservation (see note, Sect. 7.8), carefully transferring 1.063 g KHP into the LRW, stirring until it is dissolved, and then diluting to the mark with LRW (1.0 mg KHP = 0.471 mg Organic Carbon). Transfer this solution to a marked amber glass reagent bottle and cap for storage. This solution does not require refrigeration for storage and is stable for an indefinite period of time (6 months to a year). Replace the OC-PDS if the instrument system fails to pass the QCS requirements (Sect. 9.11).

7.8.4 ORGANIC CARBON CALIBRATION (OC-CAL) - At least 4 calibration concentrations and the CB (i.e., a minimum of 5 total calibration points) are required to prepare the initial calibration curve. Prepare the calibration standards over the concentration range of interest from dilutions of the OC-PDS. The calibration standards for the development of this method were prepared as specified in the table below. Calibration standards must be prepared using LRW preserved to pH ≤ 2 with concentrated acid (see note, Sect. 7.8). Filtration of the CAL standards for DOC analysis is unnecessary, since interferences from the filtration unit are monitored via the FB. Therefore, the OC-CAL may be applied to TOC or DOC determinations. The OC-CAL standards must be sparged, or otherwise treated for IC removal, like a sample following the procedure in Section 11.5.

PREPARATION OF CALIBRATION (OC-CAL) CURVE STANDARDS				
CAL Level	Initial Conc. of OC-PDS (mg/L)	Vol. of OC-PDS (mL)	Final Vol. of OC-CAL Std. (mL)	Final Conc. of OC-CAL Std. (mg/L)
CB	–	0	1000	–
1	500	1.0	1000	0.5
2	500	2.0	1000	1.0
3	500	4.0	1000	2.0
4	500	10.0	1000	5.0
5	500	20.0	1000	10.0
6 *	500	5.0	100	25.0
7 *	500	10.0	100	50.0

* Note: OC-CAL 6 - 7 are optional calibration standards for use when operating the instrument in a higher concentration range.

The calibration blank (CB) is a "0.0 mg/L OC" standard which approximates zero mg/L OC concentration plus the background carbon contributed from the LRW. The CB is stored and treated the same as all other calibration standards. When analyzed, the CB must not exceed 0.35 mg/L TOC.

7.8.5 Calibration standards may be stored at room temperature in amber glass bottles (Sect. 6.8) and/or in a dark cabinet (if clear glass used) for a period of 30 days. If stored OC-CALs are used to recalibrate the instrument during this 30 day period, the CB which has been stored with the OC-CALs must be analyzed as a sample prior to recalibration. The CB must not exceed 0.35 mg/L OC. If the CB does not meet this criteria, the CB and OC-CALs may have absorbed OC from the laboratory atmosphere and must be discarded.

7.9 COMMERCIAL SPECTROPHOTOMETER CHECK SOLUTION (COMM-SCS) - The laboratory may use a commercially prepared COMM-SCS for the purpose of checking the performance of the spectrophotometer. The analyst should purchase the COMM-SCS in the absorbance range that is commonly observed for the samples analyzed. The IN-SPEC™ optical standard and background solution for a 254 nm spectrophotometric check is NIST traceable, and is available from GFS Chemicals, PO Box 245, Powell, Ohio 43065.

    7.9.1 COMMERCIAL SPECTROPHOTOMETER BACKGROUND SOLUTION (COMM-BKS) - A background solution provided by the COMM-SCS provider that is used to correct for stabilizing agents present in the COMM-SCS.

7.10 LABORATORY PREPARED KHP-SPECTROPHOTOMETER CHECK SOLUTIONS (KHP-SCS) - The laboratory may elect to prepare a KHP based spectrophotometer check solution (KHP-SCS) for the purpose of checking the performance of the spectrophotometer at the absorbance of the average UVA sample. This requires the preparation of a buffered KHP solution having a known concentration and a known absorbance at 254 nm. The analyst should prepare the KHP-SCS that will provide an absorbance similar to the absorbance in the range (low, mid, high) of the sample analyzed. NOTE: *If the phosphate buffer reagents used below have been exposed to laboratory humidity, it is recommended that potassium dihydrogen phosphate (KH_2PO_4) and disodium hydrogen phosphate (Na_2HPO_4) be dried for 1 hour at 105°C.*

    7.10.1 KHP-SCS-BLANK - Prepare a 1-L volumetric flask containing approximately 500 mL of LRW. Transfer and dissolve 4.08 g anhydrous KH_2PO_4 and 2.84 g anhydrous Na_2HPO_4 in 500 mL. Dilute to the mark with LRW and transfer to a 1-L amber glass bottle.

    7.10.2 KHP-SCS - Prepare the KHP-SCS that will provide an absorbance similar to the absorbance of the samples analyzed. Prepare a 1-L volumetric flask containing approximately 500 mL of LRW. Transfer and dissolve 4.08 g anhydrous KH_2PO_4 and 2.84 g anhydrous Na_2HPO_4 into the 500 mL of LRW. From the example calculation, or table located below (Sect. 7.10.2.1), transfer the amount of OC-PDS (in mL) needed to produce the representative absorbance of the sample into the buffered KHP-SCS and dilute with LRW to the 1 L mark.

        7.10.2.1 KHP-SCS, CONCENTRATION CALCULATION - Standard Method 5910 B provides for a spectrophotometer check using a correlation equation which was based on the analyses of 40-samples of KHP solution.[3] The correlation formula is as follows: $UV_{254} = 0.0144\ KHP + 0.0018$. This formula may be algebraically solved for the concentration of KHP, expressed as mg/L OC, needed to produce a KHP-SCS for the observed sample absorbance as follows:

$$\text{KHP-OC conc.} = (UV_{254} - 0.0018) / 0.0144$$

Using the calculated KHP-OC concentration, determine the amount of OC-PDS (Sect. 7.8.3, 1 mL = 0.5 mg OC) needed to produce a known absorbance for the KHP-SCS. For example, if you typically run samples that have an average UVA equal to 0.08 cm^{-1}, you can calculate the KHP in the following manner:

$$5.431 \text{ KHP mg/L as OC} = (0.08 \text{ cm}^{-1} \text{ UVA}_{254} - 0.0018) / 0.0144$$

The 5.431 mg/L is the same as 5.431 mg/L KHP. It follows that to produce a 1-L KHP-SCS solution having a UVA absorbance of 0.08 cm^{-1}, you will need 10.9 mL of OC-PDS as calculated below:

$$(5.431 \text{ KHP-SCS mg/L})(1000 \text{mL/L}) / 500 \text{ OC-PDS mg/L} = 10.9 \text{ mL of OC-PDS}$$

In summary, 10.9 mL OC-PDS is needed to make a 1-L KHP-SCS solution that will have a UVA absorbance of 0.08 cm^{-1}.

Alternately, the following table, which is based on the above calculation, can be used. From this table, cross reference the amount of the OC-PDS (in mLs) needed to produce the desired UVA for the KHP-SCS. Transfer the required amount of OC-PDS into a 1-L flask and dilute to the mark with LRW.

KHP-SCS Preparation		
UVA@254nm (cm^{-1})	ORGANIC CARBON (mg/L)	OC-PDS (mL added per liter of LRW)
0.0738	5	10
0.1458	10	20
0.2898	20	40
0.4338	30	60

7.10.3 Verify that the KHP-SCS-BLANK and the KHP-SCS buffered solutions are at pH 7. Check the pH by placing a drop from the SCS bottle onto pH test paper. **Do not put the pH paper into the SCS bottle.** Placing the pH paper in the bottle will contaminate the sample with organic carbon. If this happens, the spectrophotometer check solution must be discarded and a new solution prepared in a clean bottle. If the buffered KHP-SCSs are not at a pH of 7, the solution must be discarded and a new solution made. Store these solutions at approximately ≤ 6 °C. These solutions are not preserved. In a sterile environment these solutions may be stable for a month. However, the shelf life of these solutions may be shortened as a result of microbial growth. Therefore, it is recommended that the above solutions be made fresh weekly and/or be replaced if any significant change in absorbance is noted.

8.0 SAMPLE COLLECTION, FILTRATION, AND HOLDING TIMES

NOTE: *Consult with the instrument manufacturer or operation manual for the recommended type of concentrated acid used for preservation of TOC or DOC samples. The concentrated acid used to preserve the sample is usually HCl, H_2SO_4, or H_3PO_4 depending upon the instrument operation manual recommendation. The acid used for the standards must be the same as the one used for the samples. Samples for DOC and UVA analyses may be filtered in the field using alternate apparatus technologies such as cartridges, reusable filter bodies, syringe filters, and their associated syringes, peristaltic pumps or vacuum pumps providing that the filter blank requirements are met (Sect. 9.9).*

8.1 SUVA SAMPLE COLLECTION - SUVA is determined by the analysis of a DOC sample and a UVA sample, together called the SUVA sample set. A single sample may be collected and split for the DOC and UVA analyses or two individual samples may be collected at the same time. For example: if the sample is to be determined by two separate laboratories (i.e., one lab determines UVA and a second lab determines the DOC), the sample collector may collect two representative samples for shipment. A 1-L volume is recommended for the collection of DOC and UVA samples, but other volumes may be collected depending on the sample volume needed for the filtration apparatus used by the analyzing laboratory. The SUVA sample set is collected in clean glass bottles by filling the bottle almost to the top. The sample set is **NOT preserved with acid** at the time of collection. The sample set is delivered as soon as possible to the laboratory and should arrive packed in ice or frozen gel packs. The sample set is processed by the laboratory and stored at ≤ 6 °C, until analysis. If there is no visible ice or the gel packs are completely thawed, the laboratory should report these conditions to the data user. Samples shipped that are improperly preserved, and/or do not arrive at the laboratory within 48 hrs, cannot be used to meet compliance monitoring requirements under the Safe Drinking Water Act (SDWA).

8.1.1 The DOC sample must be filtered in the field or in the laboratory within 48 hours of sample collection according to the procedure detailed in Section 11.4 prior to acidification and analysis. After filtration, the DOC sample is acidified with 1 mL of concentrated acid per 1 L of sample or the sample is preserved by drop wise adjustment to a pH ≤ 2 (Sect. 8.3). The DOC bottle is capped and inverted several times to mix the acid and is stored at ≤ 6 °C. The sample must be analyzed within 28 days from time of collection.

8.1.2 The UVA sample must be filtered in the field or in the laboratory according to the procedure detailed in Section 11.4. The sample used for the UVA determination is **not** acidified. The UVA bottle is capped and stored at ≤ 6 °C for up to 48 hours from the time of collection. The UVA sample must be analyzed within 48 hours from the time of collection.

8.2 TOC SAMPLE COLLECTION - The typical sample volume collected may vary from 40 mL to 1 L of sample. It is recommended that the sample collector coordinate the size of collection volume with the needs of the analytical laboratory. If the TOC sample is collected in a 40-mL injection vial, it is acidified to pH ≤ 2 by adding 2 drops of concentrated acid. If the TOC sample is collected in a 1-L bottle, 1 mL of concentrated acid is added or the sample is drop wise adjusted to a pH ≤ 2 (Sect. 8.3). TOC samples must be acidified at the time of collection. Cap the bottle or injection vial and invert several times to mix the acid. The sample is delivered as soon as possible to the laboratory and should arrive packed in ice or frozen gel packs. If there is no visible ice or the gel packs are completely thawed, the laboratory should report the conditions to the data user. Samples that are improperly preserved or shipped, cannot be used for compliance monitoring under the SDWA. The sample is stored at ≤ 6 °C, until analysis. Stored and preserved samples must be analyzed within 28 days from time of collection.

8.3 SAMPLE pH CHECK - The pH of the preserved sample (DOC, TOC only) or filtrate should be checked to ensure adequate acidification for the preservation. This should only be performed by an adequately trained sample collector. Check the pH by placing a drop from the sample onto pH test paper. **Do not** put the pH paper into the sample bottle. Placing the pH paper in the sample bottle will contaminate the sample with organic carbon. If this happens, the sample or filtrate must be discarded and a new sample collected.

9.0 QUALITY CONTROL

9.1 Each laboratory using this method is required to operate a formal quality control (QC) program. QC requirements for TOC include: the initial demonstration of laboratory capability (IDC) followed by regular analyses of continuing calibration checks (CCC), independent quality control samples (QCS), laboratory reagent blanks (LRB), field duplicates (FD), and laboratory fortified matrix samples (LFM). For this method, a TOC laboratory fortified blank (LFB) is the same as a CCC (Sect. 10.3) and no LFB is required. QC requirements for DOC include: the IDC followed by regular analyses of CCCs, QCSs, filter blanks (FB), LFB, FDs, and LFMs.

For laboratories analyzing both TOC and DOC samples, only the DOC IDC determination is required, as it is similar to, yet more rigorous than, the TOC IDC. The IDC must be performed the first time a new instrument is used and/or when a new analyst is trained.

QC requirements for UVA analysis include: the performance of the IDC followed by the regular analysis of spectrophotometer check solutions (SCS), FBs, and FDs. For UVA analysis, no LFB or DL determination is required.

The control of instrument background is crucial prior to the performance of the IDC. It is required that a critical evaluation be made of the instrument background [2] associated with an instrument system before proceeding with the IDC. Once an acceptable instrument background is established, it is safe to proceed with the IDC.

In summary, this section describes the minimum acceptable QC program, and laboratories are encouraged to institute additional QC practices to meet their specific needs. The laboratory must maintain records to document the quality of the data generated. All users of this method are encouraged to write their own SOPs stating exactly how their lab executes the method. A summary of QC requirements can be found in Tables 17.5 and 17.6.

9.2 INITIAL DEMONSTRATION OF CAPABILITY FOR TOC DETERMINATION

    9.2.1 INITIAL DEMONSTRATION OF LOW SYSTEM BACKGROUND - Before any samples are analyzed, and any time a new set of reagents is used, prepare a laboratory reagent blank (LRB) and demonstrate that it meets the criteria in Section 9.9.

    9.2.2 INITIAL INSTRUMENT CALIBRATION VERIFICATION - Prior to the analysis of the IDC samples, calibrate the TOC instrument as per Section 10.2. Verify calibration accuracy with the preparation and analysis of a QCS as defined in Section 9.11.

    9.2.3 INITIAL ORGANIC CARBON FLOW INJECTION MEMORY CHECK - Inject the highest OC-CAL used, followed by two injections of the LRB. If the first LRB is > 0.35 mg/L OC and the second LRB is in QC compliance (i.e., $\leq$ 0.35 mg/L OC), a memory problem is indicated. Therefore, an LRB may need to be placed after every sample. If the instrument system provides a rinse or system flush with LRB between injections, activate the event control settings and repeat this section. If the memory problem persists, then an LRB must be placed after every sample.

    9.2.4 INORGANIC CARBON REMOVAL SPARGING EFFICIENCY TEST- Various sample sparge times (3-10 minutes) and sparging flow rates have been reported for the removal of IC.[13] A multi-laboratory study reported large variations and positive bias in analyses of solutions of standards containing even small amounts of IC, demonstrating the importance of IC removal.[14] Since IC must be removed in order to reduce interferences with the TOC and

DOC quantitation, an IDC of the IC removal is performed. Please note: any manipulation of the sample may inadvertently introduce organic carbon from the apparatus.

Prepare an inorganic carbon mixture, IC-TEST solution, as specified in Section 7.8.2. Using the procedure outlined in Section 11.5, sparge at least three portions of the acidified IC-TEST solution in the same manner, and of the same volume, as field samples will be sparged. After the IC-TEST solution is treated by the IC removal apparatus, analyze the solution as an LRB for OC. The IC removal apparatus must produce an acceptable IC-TEST by meeting the LRB requirements as stated in Section 9.9. These IC removal parameters are then used for all subsequent samples.

The sparging time recommended in Section 11.5.2 is based on a sparging study with an N_2 flow rate of approximately 200 mL/min and a pH of 2.0. The following inorganic carbon concentration reduction was observed after the external sparging of a 40-mL IC-TEST solution:

IC REMOVAL SPARGE EFFICIENCY STUDY					
sparging time (minutes)	0	5	10	15	20
concentration IC (mg/L), measured as OC interference	102.5	6.11	0.611	0.049	0.044

The LRB during the above study was < 0.05 mg/L, thus a 20-minute sparge time ensured that no measurable organic carbon remained in the sample.

The above sparge efficiency table should be used only as a guide. The analyst may find that a higher flow rate may reduce the time necessary to remove the inorganic carbon to a level at or near the TOC measurements found in the LRB. The IC-TEST solution is also used to test alternate IC removal apparatus that remove IC by internal chemical treatment, alternate sparging procedures, and/or membrane IC removal. Any alternative procedure or IC removal apparatus must be tested using the IC-TEST solution and meet the LRB requirements as stated in Section 9.9.

9.2.5 INITIAL DEMONSTRATION OF ACCURACY - The initial demonstration of accuracy consists of the analysis of five (5) LFBs analyzed as samples at a concentration between 2 to 5 mg/L OC. If DOC analysis is being performed, the LFB must be filtered according to the procedure in Section 11.4. The average recovery between 2 to 5 mg/L OC must be within ±20% of the true value. If ±20% of the true value is exceeded, identify and correct the problem and repeat Sections 9.2.5 and 9.2.6.

9.2.6 INITIAL DEMONSTRATION OF PRECISION - Calculate the average precision of the replicates in the Initial Demonstration of Accuracy (Sect. 9.2.5). The RSD% must be no greater than 20%. If the RSD% exceeds 20%, identify and correct the problem and repeat Sections 9.2.5 and 9.2.6.

9.2.7 ORGANIC CARBON DETECTION LIMIT (OCDL) DETERMINATION - The OCDL determination must be conducted over at least three (3) days with a minimum of seven (n=7) replicate LFB analyses. Before conducting the initial OCDL, the OC-CAL-1 standard is used to estimate the starting concentration for the OCDL study. If DOC analyses are being performed, the low-level LFBs must be filtered according to procedure in Section 11.4 prior to analysis for the OCDL. If the instrument can easily detect the OC-CAL-1 standard, the analyst should lower the concentration to a level so that the LFB produces a signal 2 to 5 times the background noise level of the instrument. It is recommended that the LFB be fortified somewhere between 0.1 to 0.5 mg/L OC. All available instrument digits are carried for the OCDL calculation. After completion of the OCDL, the calculation is rounded up or down according to Standard Method 1050 B.[15] The final result is reported in units used for the TOC or DOC procedure and recorded to two significant figures in the instrument log book. Calculate the OCDL using the equation:

$$\text{Organic Carbon Detection Limit} = S t_{(n-1,\, 1-\text{alpha}\, =\, 0.99)}$$

where:

$t_{(n-1, 1-\text{alpha} = 0.99)}$ = Student's t value for the 99% confidence level with n-1 degrees of freedom (t = 3.14 for 7 replicates)
n = number of replicates, and
S = standard deviation of replicate analyses.

If the initial OCDL exceeds 0.35 mg/L or the mean recovery of the LFB used in the OCDL determination exceeds ± 50% of the true value, then the OCDL determination must be repeated.

9.3 INITIAL DEMONSTRATION OF CAPABILITY FOR DOC DETERMINATION

9.3.1 Perform Sections 9.2.1 through 9.2.4 as prescribed for TOC.

9.3.2 INITIAL DEMONSTRATION OF FILTER MEMBRANE SUITABILITY - Filter membranes are capable of affecting DOC and UVA analyses either by desorption (leaching) of DOC and UV-absorbing materials from the filters to the samples, or by adsorption (uptake) of DOC and UV-absorbing materials from the samples onto the filters. Filter membranes selected for DOC and UVA measurements must not desorb nor adsorb significant DOC and UV-absorbing materials. Desorption is minimized by pre-washing selected filters as described in Section 9.3.2.2. Adsorption is minimized by filtering a portion of the sample to waste before sample collection as described in Section 9.3.2.3. Because the filtration of relatively turbid samples may cause filters to clog, pre-filtration may be necessary and pre-filter preparation is described in Section 9.3.2.1. Due to the possibility of lot-to-lot variations in the levels of contamination or adsorption, it is recommended that for each filter lot, the user determine the amount of LRW needed to wash the filters and the amount of sample that needs to be filtered and discarded prior to collection of filtrate (filter-to-waste volume). A minimum of three filters (from each new lot) should be cleaned and checked for desorption/adsorption prior to using the filters for actual samples. This evaluation must be repeated when filters are purchased from another manufacturer or when the type of filter being used is changed.

9.3.2.1 PRE-FILTER PREPARATION - If the analyst anticipates that the UVA and DOC sample will clog the 0.45-µm pore size filter membrane before enough filtrate can be collected, glass fiber pre-filters without organic binders may be used. Karanfil et al [10] suggested cleaning the pre-filter by heating to 550 °C for one hour, cooling to room temperature, then washing it with 500 mL of LRW. A 25-mL filter-to-waste volume (Sect. 9.3.2.3) was also recommended. The pre-filters must be demonstrated as acceptable using the procedures described below in Sections 9.3.2.2 and 9.3.2.3. Depending on the design of the filter apparatus, the analyst may be able to insert a pre-filter into the filter apparatus. The pre-filter and filter apparatus could then be washed as a unit, following the procedure in Section 9.3.2.2. Prefilter adsorption and desorption may also be tested separately from the filter membrane.

9.3.2.2 FILTER CLEANING - UV-absorbing materials and DOC are removed from the filter and filter apparatus by passing LRW through the filter. The volume of LRW required depends on the type and disc size of the filter. For the filter apparatus used to generate the data in this method, three successive rinses of 250 mL each (for a total of 750 mL) removed UV-absorbing materials and DOC that could leach from the filter and apparatus. (The Karanfil [10] study found that a 500 mL wash was sufficient to prepare the 47-mm disk filters recommended in their study for DOC samples and a wash of 100 mL was sufficient for filters used solely to prepare UVA samples.) Acceptable cleaning is demonstrated by analyzing filter blanks (Sects. 11.4.3, 11.6) and meeting the criteria in Section 9.9. The volume of LRW required to obtain acceptable filter blanks is then used to clean filters for analyses of all samples (Sect. 11.4). Filters that cannot be cleaned to meet the referenced criteria must not be used in the preparation of DOC and UVA samples.

9.3.2.3 FILTER-TO-WASTE VOLUME DETERMINATION - In order to minimize the loss of sample onto the filter by adsorption, a portion of the sample must be used to saturate the adsorption sites on the filter after it is cleaned according to Section 9.3.2.2. The amount of sample filtrate that must be discarded prior to collecting filtrate for DOC and/or UVA analyses will vary depending upon the type and size of filter and the volume should be minimized in order to prevent filter clogging. A 25-mL filter-to-waste volume was recommended when using the hydrophilic polyethersulfone and hydrophilic polypropylene filters of 47-mm disc size studied by Karanfil et al [10] based on evaluations using low-turbidity model waters prepared from preconcentrated humic and fulvic materials.

In this method, a low-turbidity (i.e., TOC = DOC) finished water sample can be used in the filter-to-waste determination. For laboratories that are analyzing samples from a variety of sources, the selected water should have a TOC concentration in the range of 1 to 3 mg/L. For laboratories that only analyze samples from one source, the selected water should be a finished water with the lowest TOC that is generally observed (NOTE: Depending on the quality of the source water, this could be water with a TOC concentration much higher than the 1 to 3 mg/L recommended for laboratories that are analyzing samples from a variety of sources.)

A series of at least three filtrates are collected in separate containers for the filter-to-waste volume determination. The volume of each filtrate is determined based on the minimum volume required to make an analytical determination. For example, if the DOC analysis requires 30 mL, then a series of at least three successive 30-mL filtrates should be collected. For UVA, three successive 10-mL filtrates can be collected. If DOC and UVA analyses are to be performed on the same filtrate, then the volume of each filtrate should be adjusted to provide the minimum volume necessary to accommodate both analyses (in the above example, three successive 40-mL washes).

Each filtrate is analyzed according to the procedure in Section 11 and the concentration is compared to the concentration of the unfiltered sample. When the concentration of the filtrate is within ± 15% of the concentration measured in the unfiltered sample, then the recommended filter-to-waste volume is the sum of the volumes of that filtrate and any previous filtrates in the series. For example, if the unfiltered sample has a TOC concentration of 3.5 mg/L and the filtrate series (each filtrate = 30 mL) have concentrations of 2.3, 3.2, and 3.4 mg/L, then a minimum of 60 mL of sample should be filtered-to-waste prior to collecting filtrate for DOC analyses. It is recommended that the filter-to-waste volume be determined by performing this test on at least three filters from each lot and averaging the results. **Filters that require large volumes of filter-to-waste should be avoided**, because they will be more subject to clogging prior to the collection of the necessary volume of filtrate for analysis. The filter-to-waste volume that is determined in this section must be used in the filtration procedure described in Section 11.4.4.

9.3.3 Perform Sections 9.2.5 through 9.2.7 using filtered LFBs. The LFBs must be prepared using the same procedure used to prepare samples (Sect. 11.4).

9.4 INITIAL DEMONSTRATION OF CAPABILITY FOR UVA DETERMINATION

9.4.1 INITIAL CHECK OF SPECTROPHOTOMETER PERFORMANCE - The UV Spectrophotometer must be checked annually for 0 % transmittance, wavelength accuracy, stray radiant energy, accuracy and linearity, and optical alignment. It is recommended that the instrument performance be verified through the manufacturer or a scientific instrument service company. If independent verification of performance is not feasible, the laboratory may acquire a certified spectrophotometric filter set and conduct the evaluation. Wavelength verification is made using certified spectrophotometric filter sets with values traceable to NIST. Using the filter set, test two wavelengths between 220 and 340 nm. The instrument performance should be recorded in the instrument log and be used to monitor the spectrophotometer performance over time. Follow the instrument manufacturer's operation manual when measuring the acceptable wavelength transmittance limits.

9.4.2 Verify the spectrophotometer performance according to the procedure as outlined in Section 10.4.

9.4.3 Conduct the filter membrane suitability study described in Section 9.3.2 for UVA.

9.5 CONTINUING CALIBRATION CHECK (CCC) - With each analysis batch, analyze a Low-CCC at or below the MRL (Sect. 9.10) prior to TOC or DOC sample analysis. Subsequent CCCs are analyzed after every ten samples and after the last sample. The concentrations should be rotated to cover the instrument calibration range. A Mid-CCC is required during every analysis batch. Acceptance criteria are as follows: Low-

CCC, ± 50% of true value; Mid-CCC, ± 20% of true value; High-CCC, ± 15% of true value, see Section 10.3 for concentrations.

9.6 FIELD DUPLICATE (FD) - Within each analysis batch, a minimum of one set of field duplicates must be analyzed (FD1 and FD2). Sample homogeneity and the chemical nature of the sample matrix can affect analyte recovery and the quality of the data. Duplicate sample analyses serve as a check on sampling and laboratory precision. Two samples are collected at the field site and are treated exactly alike.

    9.6.1 Calculate the relative percent difference (RPD) for duplicate measurements (FD1 and FD2) using the equation:

$$RPD = \frac{|FD1 - FD2|}{(FD1 + FD2)/2} * 100$$

    9.6.2 Relative percent difference for field duplicates having an average concentration of ≥ 2 mg/L OC should fall in the range of $\leq 20\%$ RPD. If field duplicates in this concentration range exhibit an RPD greater than 20%, results should be flagged and the cause for the greater difference (e.g. incomplete IC removal or matrix interference), investigated. UVA readings should be $\leq 10\%$ RPD. NOTE: *Greater variability may be observed for samples with OC approaching the OCDL.*

9.7 LABORATORY FORTIFIED BLANK (LFB) - Within each DOC analysis batch, analyze an aliquot of reagent water or other blank matrix which has been fortified with KHP at a concentration of 1-5 mg/L OC. Recovery for the LFB must be within ±20% of the true value. One LFB is required with each DOC analysis batch. For the DOC analysis, an LFB is subjected to the same preparation and analysis as a sample, including filtration (Sect. 11.4). The LFB is not determined for the TOC or UVA measurements.

9.8 LABORATORY FORTIFIED MATRIX (LFM) - Within each TOC or DOC analysis batch, an aliquot of one field sample is fortified with an aliquot of the OC-PDS (Sect. 7.8.3). The spike concentration used should result in an increase in the LFM concentration of 50 to 200% of its measured or expected concentration. Over time, samples from all routine sample sources should be fortified. For DOC analysis, the LFM is filtered prior to acidification and analysis.

    9.8.1 Calculate the percent spike recovery (%REC) using the equation:

$$\%REC = \frac{(A - B)}{C} * 100$$

where
A = measured concentration in the fortified sample
B = measured concentration in the unfortified sample, and
C = fortification concentration.

9.8.2 Recoveries may exhibit a matrix dependence. If the LFM recovery falls outside of 70 to 130% for any fortified concentration, the analyst should suspect that inorganic carbon was not properly removed (Sect. 11.5) from the sample or that contamination or matrix interference exists (Sect. 4) and can not be removed. If the source of the poor recovery can not be identified, the analyst should label the sample report "suspect/contamination or matrix interference" to inform the data user that the sample data quality is questionable but should not be rejected. Failure to meet the recovery criteria after repeated sampling may suggest that the sample matrix may need further study.

9.9 LABORATORY REAGENT BLANK (LRB) AND FILTER BLANK (FB) - Within each analysis batch, a minimum of one LRB must be analyzed. For DOC and UVA analysis, the FB serves as the LRB. If more than one lot of filters is used in a DOC or UVA analytical batch, a FB must be analyzed for each lot. The analyst should be aware that additional filter blanks, up to one for each sample, are required by some regulations (e.g., *40 CFR 141.131(d)(4)(i)*).

The LRB or FB is used to assess contamination from the laboratory environment and background contamination from the reagents used in sample processing and is treated exactly the same as a sample. The volume of the FB must be the same as the sample volume. If UVA is to be determined, the FB (UVA-FB) must have an absorbance of ≤ 0.01 cm^{-1} UVA. The LRB and/or the FB (DOC-FB) must be ≤ 0.35 mg/L OC. If 0.35 mg/L OC or 0.01 cm^{-1} UVA is exceeded, background carbon or reagent contamination should be suspected. The cause for significant changes in the LRB or FB value must be identified and any determined source of contamination must be eliminated. For the FB, this may mean redetermination of filter membrane suitability (Sect. 9.3.2). The cause of the contamination and the corrective action used to remedy the problem is then recorded in the instrument log for future reference.

9.10 MINIMUM REPORTING LEVEL (MRL) - The OCDL should not be used as the MRL. For TOC analysis, it is recommended that an MRL be established no lower than the mean LRB measurement plus 3σ, or two times the mean LRB measurement, whichever is greater. For DOC analysis, the FB is substituted for the LRB. This value should be calculated over a period of time, to reflect variability in the blank measurements. **Although the lowest calibration standard for OC may be below the MRL, the MRL for OC must never be established at a concentration lower than the lowest OC calibration standard.**

9.11 QUALITY CONTROL SAMPLE (QCS) - During the analysis of the IDC (Sects. 9.2, 9.3), each time new OC-PDS solutions are prepared (Sect. 7.8.3), or at least quarterly, analyze a QCS from a source different from the source of the calibration standards. The QCS is used to provide an independent verification of the method and the TOC instrument system. To verify the stock or calibration solutions by comparison with the QCS, dilute the calibration solution and QCS to a concentration in the mid range of the calibration curve (approx. 1 - 5 mg/L TOC) in the same manner that the OC-CAL standards are made (Sect. 7.8.4). Acceptable verification of the calibration is made when the means of 3 analyses for both the calibration solution and QCS, having a concentration range between 1 to 5 mg/L OC, agree to within ±20% of the true value. If the measured QCS concentration is not within ±20% of the true value, the calibration solution must be remade and/or the source of the problem must be determined and corrected. Analysis of the QCS only applies to TOC and DOC determination.

9.12 SPECTROPHOTOMETER CHECK REQUIREMENT - The performance of the spectrophotometer is initially demonstrated using the procedure in Section 9.4.1. The day-to-day performance of the spectrophotometer is checked using KHP-SCS (Sect. 7.10) or a commercially available SCS (COMM-SCS, Sect. 7.9) according to the procedure in Section 10.4.

10.0 CALIBRATION AND STANDARDIZATION

10.1 INSTRUMENT SET UP AND OPTIMIZATION - Prior to calibrating the TOC instrument, clean the instrument system with carbon dioxide free water and sparge reagents with ultra high purity reagent gas as specified by the instrument manufacturer to remove background carbon dioxide. NOTE: *TOC Instrument 1 does not require reagent gas for operation.* Monitor the instrument background carbon dioxide levels for at least 30 minutes or until the background signal reaches the manufacturer's recommended level. The instrument should have a stable background and be free from drift caused by CO_2 contaminated gas or leaks in the system. Adjust instrument temperature, reagent gas and reagent pump flow settings according to the manufacturer's operation manual. Some instruments may require reagent priming runs to clean the flow injection system and reduce carbon background. After the instrument is judged to be stable, load the auto-injector or prepare to manually inject four LRB samples and start the analysis. The data collected from the first injection of LRB is discarded and is considered a system cleanup blank. The next three LRB injections should produce consecutive readings that fall within 20% of their mean. If these conditions are met, the instrument is ready for calibration. If not, use the OC-CAL-1 standard and repeat this section. If the three injections of OC-CAL-1 do not produce consecutive readings that fall within 20% of their mean, the instrument is not ready to operate and maintenance must be performed according to the instrument operation manual before proceeding.

10.2 CALIBRATION CURVE - A new calibration curve is generated when fresh standards are made (Sect. 7.8.4) or when CCCs fall out of QC limits (Sect. 10.3). Use a CB and at least four OC-CAL standards that span the concentration range of the samples to be analyzed. For example, if the samples to be analyzed are low in concentration (a range falling between 0.5 to 5 mg/L OC), prepare a calibration blank and a minimum of four TOC calibration standards (CB, OC-CAL 1 - 4, see Sect. 7.8.4). The lowest concentration calibration standard must be at or below the MRL, which may depend on system sensitivity. Add an additional 40 μL of H_3PO_4, HCl, or H_2SO_4, depending upon instrument requirements (Sect. 8.0), to the 40-mL injection vial(s). Sparge the calibration standards using the IC removal procedure in Section 11.5 prior to calibrating the instrument. Inject the standards from low to high concentration and calibrate the instrument. Be careful not to extend the calibration range over too wide of a concentration range as flow injection memory may cause analytical error (Sect. 9.2.3). The optional OC-CAL 6 - 7 may be used when operating the instrument in a higher concentration range.

NOTE: *For instruments that have an internal calibration setting, the calibration is checked by comparing the five point calibration curve with the internal calibration point. If the five point calibration curve does not agree with the internal calibration using the CCC criteria in Section 10.3, the internal calibration of TOC instrument must be reset by the manufacturer or adjusted by the analyst, following the manufacturer's operation manual.*

10.2.1 With the instrument in the ready mode, initiate the automated instrument calibration routine as per the instrument manufacturer's operation manual. The computer generated calibration curve must have $r^2 \geq 0.993$ before proceeding with analyses. Ideally the instrument calibration should be $r^2 \geq 0.9995$ for best results. After the instrument system has been calibrated, verify the calibration using the Continuing Calibration Check (CCC, Sect. 10.3) and QCS (Sect. 9.11).

10.2.2 Save the data from the initial calibration curve and record it in the laboratory notebook or instrument log. The initial calibration curve serves as a historical reference so that future calibrations curves can be compared to determine if the slope or sensitivity of calibration has changed. If the slope or sensitivity of the instrument changes such that QC requirements cannot be met, consult the instrument manual or lab SOP for corrective action, which may include instrument maintenance and recalibration.

10.3 CONTINUING CALIBRATION CHECK (CCC) - Demonstration and documentation of continuing calibration is required and must meet the requirements listed below. The CCC solutions are made up weekly or just prior to a sample run and are prepared in the same manner as the OC-CALs (Sect. 7.8.4). An analysis batch begins with the analysis of a Low-CCC. CCCs are analyzed every 10 samples and must also include a

Mid-CCC. Subsequent CCCs should alternate between low, medium, and high concentrations, and must end the analysis batch. In summary, at least one Low-CCC and one Mid-CCC is analyzed with each analysis batch in order to verify the calibration curve. It is recommended that low, mid, and high CCCs be used to verify the calibration curve over time.

- 10.3.1 **Low-CCC** - the concentration range may vary from as low as 2 times the OCDL up to 0.7 mg/L OC. The Low-CCC is used to verify the low end of the calibration and must be at or below the MRL, which may depend on system sensitivity. The recovery for the Low-CCC must be within $\pm$ 50% of the true value.

- 10.3.2 **Mid-CCC** - the concentration is varied between 1.0 mg/L to 5.0 mg/L OC. The purpose of this CCC is to verify the precision and accuracy at the calibration range where critical source water treatment decisions are made. The Mid-CCC concentration may be varied to meet changing regulatory requirements. The Mid-range CCC must be within $\pm 20\%$ of the true value. If it is not, the TOC instrument system must be recalibrated.

- 10.3.3 **High-CCC** - the concentration range is varied between 5 to 50 mg/L OC. The selection of the High-CCC should be near the concentration of the highest OC-CAL standard used. The purpose of this CCC is to bracket the concentration the samples that are typically analyzed and to verify the upper range of the calibration curve. High-CCC must be within $\pm 15\%$ of the true value. If it is not, the TOC instrument system must be recalibrated.

10.4 SPECTROPHOTOMETER PERFORMANCE CHECK - The performance of the spectrophotometer is initially demonstrated using the procedure in Section 9.4.1. The day-to-day performance of the spectrophotometer is checked using KHP-SCS (Sect. 7.10) or a commercially available SCS (COMM-SCS, Sect. 7.9) prior to analyzing any UVA samples using the procedure described below.

- 10.4.1 Using a transfer pipet fill the spectrophotometer cell with the COMM-BKS or KHP-SCS-BLANK (Sects. 7.9.1, 7.10.1). Use this solution to zero the spectrophotometer.

- 10.4.2 After the spectrophotometer is zeroed, empty the cell, clean with LRW, rinse with methanol, dry with N_2 or reagent grade air, and fill it with the KHP-SCS or COMM-SCS.

- 10.4.3 Read the UVA of the KHP-SCS or COMM-SCS. The reading must be within 10% of the expected absorbance value. Record the absorbance of the KHP-SCS or COMM-SCS in the spectrophotometer instrument logbook. Empty the cell, clean with LRW, rinse with methanol, and dry with N_2 or reagent grade air.

10.4.4 If the SCS absorbance criteria stated above cannot be met, discard the COMM-SCS or the KHP-SCS and purchase new COMM-SCS or remake the KHP-SCS. Repeat Section 10.4.

11.0 PROCEDURE

11.1 TOC/DOC SAMPLE INTEGRITY EVALUATION - It is important to analyze a TOC or DOC sample as directly and as soon as possible. Sample handling and preparation should be minimized. Upon receiving the sample from the field, the analyst must determine if the sample was treated and stored according to instructions found in Section 8.

11.2 OPTIONAL TREATMENT FOR TOC/DOC SAMPLE MATRIX LOSS - Aquatic humic substances precipitate at pH below 2 [16], and may move to glass vessel walls or instrument tubing. If the analyst suspects that humic substances have precipitated (which sometimes occurs in blackwaters)[14] or flocked to the bottom of the sample container, the sample is degassed by sparging to remove IC as directed in Section 11.5. The sample is then split into two portions. One portion is left at a pH ≤2, and the pH of the second portion is adjusted to pH 5 to 7 in order to increase the solubility of hydrophobic matter in the sample. Both samples are allowed to sit capped for ½ hour before further sample processing. These samples are treated in the same manner as field duplicates (FD), Section 9.6. The results of both split samples and corresponding pH values should be reported to the data user.

11.3 TOC SAMPLE PREPARATION - Remove the TOC sample from cold storage and allow the sample to come to room temperature. Determine if the sample has been preserved by acidification to a pH ≤2 by placing some drops on pH paper or by pouring some of the sample into a small beaker and checking it with a glass or solid-state pH electrode. **Do Not** put the pH paper or electrode into the sample bottle. If the pH is greater than 2, discard the sample.

11.3.1 TYPICAL TOC SAMPLE PRE-TREATMENT - Samples that appear to be low in particulate and suspended material are generally transferred directly to the 40-mL injection vial. If the sample appears to contain sediment or floating material, allow the sample to sit for a minute or two to allow sediment material to settle back to the bottom of the bottle. After allowing the sample to settle, transfer the sample from the middle of the bottle using a disposable pipet to the injection vial. Add 40 μL of H_3PO_4, HCl, or H_2SO_4 depending upon instrument requirements (Sect. 8.0) to the 40-mL injection vial and label it.

11.3.2 Proceed to Section 11.5, for IC removal.

11.4 SUVA SAMPLE PREPARATION - If SUVA is not being determined, proceed to Section 11.5. The SUVA determination consists of paired sample analyses composed of a DOC sample and a UVA sample. DOC and UVA samples may be taken from the same bottle, or may be taken from separate field duplicate bottles. Remove the DOC and UVA sample(s) from cold storage and allow them to come to room temperature. The laboratory is required to document any use of alternative filters, apparatus (see note, Sect. 6.1), or changes in the SUVA sample preparation procedure. All QC requirements (Sect. 9) must be met.

   11.4.1 Samples for DOC and UVA analysis are NOT acidified in the field. The DOC sample is acidified after filtration as described below and the UVA sample is not acidified at all. Determine if the sample(s) was accidentally preserved by placing a few drops from the sample on pH paper or by pouring some of the sample into a small beaker and checking it with a glass or solid-state pH electrode. **Do Not** put the pH paper or electrode into the sample bottle. Placing the pH paper or electrode into the sample bottle will contaminate the sample solution with organic carbon. If this happens, the sample must be discarded. If the UVA sample pH is ≤ 2, check to make sure that the sample is actually for the UVA determination. It is possible that this sample is a TOC or filtered DOC sample and was mislabeled as a UVA sample. If the sample set was not mislabeled or switched but accidentally preserved, the sample must be discarded. The analyst must check the date and time of collection to ensure that the sample holding times listed in Section 8.1 have been met.

   11.4.2 Filter Cleaning - Cleaning the filter apparatus, including the filter, removes trace organic compounds that may have been left behind in the manufacturing process. This cleaning must be done immediately prior to sample filtration. Rinse the filter with LRW, using the cleaning procedure used to determine filter membrane suitability (Sect. 9.3.2.2), including the cleaning of the pre-filter if a pre-filter is necessary.

   11.4.3 Filter Blank (FB) - Use a clean filter apparatus (prepared in Sect. 11.4.2) and filter an aliquot of LRW into an injection vial for the DOC analysis and another aliquot of LRW into a vial for UVA analysis (Figure 1). FB volume must be the same as the sample volume collected in Section 11.4.4. During the development of this method, approximately 250 mL of LRW was filtered and aliquots were poured into two 40-mL injection vials and labeled as the DOC and UVA FBs. If the DOC and UVA analyses are coming from two separate bottles, a filter apparatus will be needed for each bottle and an FB should be prepared from each apparatus. Add 40 µL of H_3PO_4, HCl, or H_2SO_4 (as required by the various instrument types, Sect. 8.0) to the 40-mL DOC-FB injection vial. **Do not acidify** the UVA-FB injection vial. These vials are paired with the respective SUVA sample and retained for DOC-FB and UVA-FB analyses.

11.4.4 Sample Preparation - Reassemble the filter apparatus. Pour enough sample onto the filter to saturate any adsorption sites, as determined according to the filter-to-waste procedure in Section 9.3.2.3. Apply vacuum until no visible water remains on the filter. Remove the vacuum, swirl the apparatus with sample filtrate, disassemble, and discard the sample filtrate rinse. Reassemble the filter apparatus and pour an additional aliquot of sample into the top of the filter apparatus. Attach the vacuum and retain the filtrate. Pour one aliquot into a 40-mL injection vial and label it to identify it as the DOC sample. Pour a second aliquot into a 40-mL injection vial and label it to identify it as the UVA sample. Add 40 μL of H_3PO_4, HCl, or H_2SO_4 to the 40-mL DOC injection vial. **Do not acidify** the UVA injection vial. As with the DOC and UV FBs (Sect. 11.4.3), separate filter apparatus may be used for the DOC and UVA samples, in which case the filtrate need not be split into two aliquots. For a sample that is difficult to filter, an additional filter apparatus or the optional pre-filter insert apparatus may be used. The use of additional filters may require the collection of additional FBs, collected as specified in Section 11.4.3. The resulting additional DOC-FB, UVA-FB sample filtrates are collected, their volumes composited and then placed into their respective injection vials.

11.5 INORGANIC CARBON REMOVAL - **All OC-CALs, TOC and DOC samples, DOC-FBs, and LRBs must be treated to remove IC prior to OC analysis. UVA samples and UVA-FBs are not sparged with nitrogen gas or otherwise treated to remove IC prior to analysis** (See Figure 2). The laboratory is required to document any use of alternative IC removal apparatus (Sects. 6.9, 11.5.2) or changes in the IC removal procedure. All quality control requirements (Sect. 9.2.4) must be met.
NOTE: *If a sparging apparatus is used, it should be isolated from the organic laboratory and be free of organic contaminants.*

11.5.1 CLEANING SPARGING APPARATUS: Before initial use and immediately after each use, the sparging apparatus must be cleaned. With the nitrogen turned off, dip the stainless steel needles in a 40-mL injection vial containing dilute acid (40 μL H_3PO_4, HCL, or H_2SO_4 per 40 mL LRW). Take the needles out of the dilute acid and turn the nitrogen back on to flush out any residual dilute acid. If disposable pipettes are used as part of the sparging apparatus, discard the pipettes after each use instead of attempting to clean and reuse them.

11.5.2 SPARGING PROCEDURE: Submerge the apparatus needles used to sparge the samples near the bottom of the 40-mL sample injection vial. Data generated for this method were generated by externally sparging the acidified samples with nitrogen gas, at 100 to 200 mL/minute, for 20 minutes per 40-mL sample injection vial. Some instrument companies provide optional inorganic carbon removal apparatus that may produce an efficient means for the removal of IC. The laboratory must demonstrate sparging efficiency by the performance of the IC removal sparging efficiency test (Sect. 9.2.4) and meeting the LRB requirements as stated in Section 9.9.

11.6 SAMPLE ASSAY

11.6.1 TOC/DOC Sample Analysis - This is accomplished by placing into the injection vial tray a series of 40-mL injection vials usually containing any or all of the following types of samples: LRB, DOC-FB, CB, OC-CAL(s), CCC s (Low, Mid or High concentration), field samples, FD1 & FD2, LRB between samples if needed as specified in Section 9.2.3, LFB, LFM, and the QCS. The DOC-FB maximum allowable background concentration is 0.35 mg/L OC. The injection tray is placed into the instrument, the run is initiated, and the results of analyses are recorded.

11.6.2 UVA ANALYSES - If the spectrophotometer performance meets the SCS absorbance criteria as stated in Section 10.4, fill the cell with LRW and zero the instrument. Rinse and fill the cell with LRW from a second source. Verify $UVA \leq 0.01$ cm^{-1} for second source LRW. Next fill the cell with the UVA-FB and read the absorbance. The UVA-FB's maximum allowable background absorbance is 0.01 cm^{-1} UVA. If 0.01 cm^{-1} UVA for the UVA-FB is exceeded, the cause must be identified and any determined source of contamination must be eliminated. The spectrophotometer performance must then be rechecked (Sect. 10.4). The laboratory should also check the initial zero each time 10 samples have been read. Rinse the spectrophotometer cell with a small amount of the UVA sample or UVA-FB by directly pipetting or pouring the sample into the spectrophotometer cell and discarding the rinse. Refill the spectrophotometer cell, carefully clean the cell window, and place in the spectrophotometer cell holder. Alternatively, flow cells maybe used, filled and flushed as needed. Measure the UVA and record. If field duplicates are collected, the FD1 & FD2 sample filtrates are also read and recorded.

12.0   DATA ANALYSIS AND CALCULATION

12.1 TOC DIRECT READING: The TOC concentration is calculated by the automated instrument system's software. Follow the instrument manufacturer's operation manual when making instrument response adjustments for instrument system blank corrections. The TOC calculation assumes that the sample has been properly preserved, that only a trace amount of IC remains following the IC removal procedure, and that any remaining IC will not contribute to the TOC measurement and result in a calculation error. Some instrument systems calculate TOC from the difference of the total carbon (TC) minus the IC. The analyst is reminded that the IC in the sample is removed prior to sample analysis. Therefore, the reported TC is equal to, and the same as, the TOC value (TOC =TC) and is read directly from the instrument's computer or printout.

12.2 SUVA CALCULATION: Follow the instrument manufacturer's operation manual instructions when making instrument response adjustments for instrument system blank correction. As in the above TOC calculation, the analyst is reminded that the IC of the DOC sample is removed prior to analysis. After filtration, the TOC instrument value is equal to the DOC. The SUVA is then calculated from the DOC & UVA data that results from the procedure as described above (Sects. 11.6.1, 11.6.2). The UVA of the sample in cm^{-1} is divided by the DOC of the sample, multiplied by 100 cm/M and either reported in units of L/mg-M or as "SUVA". The SUVA is calculated as follows:

$$SUVA~(L/mg\text{-}M) = UVA(cm^{-1}) / DOC~(mg/L) * 100~cm/M$$

UVA Calculation: $UVA = A/d$

where:

UVA = The calculated UV absorbance of the sample in absorbance units (cm^{-1}).

A = The measured UV absorbance at 254 nm of the sample that is filtered through a 0.45-μm filter media.

d = The quartz cell path length in cm.

NOTE: *A Filter Blank (FB) is used to monitor background carbon contamination (Sect. 11.4.3) and is not subtracted from the DOC and UVA measurements.*

12.3 Calculations should utilize all available digits of precision, but final reported concentrations should be rounded to two significant figures (one digit of uncertainty). The final calculation is rounded up or down according to Standard Method 1050B.[15]

13.0 METHOD PERFORMANCE

NOTE: *Data presented in Section 17 are from single-laboratory determinations. All available digits were used for calculation and the calculations were rounded prior to entry in the tables. The data were reported to as many as three significant figures to give the reader a better understanding of method performance.*

13.1 Table 17.1 summarizes the 3-day organic carbon detection limit (OCDL) study for five TOC instruments systems. The DOC determination ranged from 0.02 to 0.08 mg/L OCDL and the TOC determination ranged from 0.04 to 0.12 mg/L OCDL. All source water samples reported in Section 13 and the Section 17 Tables were sparged for 20 minutes to remove inorganic carbon interferences.

13.2 Table 17.2 and associated sub-tables illustrate the single instrument precision and accuracy for each of the five TOC instrument technologies.

13.3 Tables 17.3 and 17.4 illustrate the instrument differences and performances for five TOC instruments analyzing seven different source water matrices.

13.4 In all cases, the TOC instruments had difficulty in analyzing the Saint Leon well water. The Saint Leon well water had a moderately high inorganic carbon content of approximately 100 mg/L IC, and a low organic carbon content of 0.2 to 0.6 mg/L OC. The Saint Leon well water organic carbon content was near the organic carbon detection limit. The low OC concentration produced the greatest differences between instrument responses. For low TOC samples with high IC, differences between instrument responses may be more apparent due to possible IC interference.

13.5 The TOC, DOC and SUVA procedures of this method are dependent on the operation manual for the TOC instrument system and the UV spectrophotometer as provided by the respective instrument manufacturers. However, all performance criteria and quality control requirements described in this method, as summarized in Tables 17.5 and 17.6, must be met.

14.0 POLLUTION PREVENTION

14.1 Pollution prevention encompasses any technique that reduces or eliminates the quantity or toxicity of waste at the point of generation. Numerous opportunities for pollution prevention exist in laboratory operations. The EPA has established a preferred hierarchy of environmental management techniques that places pollution prevention as the management option of first choice. Whenever feasible, laboratory personnel should use pollution prevention techniques to address their waste generation. When wastes cannot be feasibly reduced at the source, the Agency recommends recycling as the next best option.

14.2 For information about pollution prevention that may be applicable to laboratories and research institutions, consult *Less is Better: Laboratory Chemical Management for Waste Reduction*, available from the American Chemical Society's Department of Government Relations and Science Policy, 1155 16th Street N.W., Washington D.C. 20036, (202)872-4477.

14.3 For recycle information, contact the US EPA, Pollution Prevention and WasteWise program, http://www.epa.gov/wastewise/ .

15.0 WASTE MANAGEMENT

15.1 The U.S. Environmental Protection Agency requires that laboratory waste management practices be conducted consistent with all applicable rules and regulations. The Agency urges laboratories to protect the air, water, and land by minimizing and controlling all releases from hoods and bench operations, complying with the letter and spirit of any sewer discharge permits and regulations, and by complying with all solid and hazardous waste regulations, particularly the hazardous waste identification rules and land disposal restrictions. For further information on waste management, consult *The Waste Management Manual for Laboratory Personnel*, available from the American Chemical Society at the address listed in Section 14.2.

15.2 The laboratory should consult with local authorities prior to disposal of any waste to publicly owned treatment works (POTW) and receive permission for that disposal.

16.0 REFERENCES

1. Glaser, J. A.; Foerst, D. L.; McKee G. D.; Quave, S. A.; Budde, W. L. Trace Analyses for Wastewaters. *Environ. Sci. Technol.* **1981**, *15* (12), 1426-1434.

2. Benner, R.; Storm, M. A Critical Evaluation of the Analytical Blank Associated with DOC Measurements by High-Temperature Catalytic Oxidation. *Mar. Chem.* **1993**, *41*, 153-160.

3. Standard Method 5910B: Ultraviolet Absorption Method. In *Standard Methods for the Examination of Water and Wastewater,* Eaton, A. D.; Clesceri, L. S.; Greenberg, A. E., Eds.; American Public Health Association; Washington, DC, 1995; 19th ed.

4. Aiken, G.R. Chloride Interference in the Analysis of Dissolved Organic Carbon by the Wet Oxidation Method. *Environ. Sci. Technol.* **1992**, *26* (12), 2435-2439.

5. Sakamoto, T.; Miyasaka, T. TOC Analysis Study Confirming the Accuracy of a Method for Measuring TOC by Wet Oxidation. *Ultrapure Water* **1987**, 24-31.

6. Potter, B. B.; Wimsatt, J. C. Preprints of Extended Abstracts, Vol 42 (1), 223rd National Meeting of the American Chemical Society, Orlando, FL, April 7-11, 2002; American Chemical Society Division of Environmental Chemistry: Cape Girardeau, MO, 2002; Paper 60, 559-564.

7. Aiken, G.; Kaplan, L. A.; Weishaar, J. Assessment of Relative Accuracy in the Determination of Organic Matter Concentrations in Aquatic Systems. *J. Environ. Monit.* **2002**, *4*, 70-74.

8. American Chemical Society, Committee on Chemical Safety. *Safety in Academic Chemistry Laboratories, Vol. 2, Accident Prevention for Faculty and Administrators, 7th ed.*; American Chemical Society: Washington, DC, 2003.

9. Occupational Exposure to Hazardous Chemicals in Laboratories. *Code of Federal Regulations*, Part 1910.1450, Title 29, **2001**.

10. Karanfil, T.; Erdogan, I.; Schlautman, M. A. Selecting Filter Membranes for Measuring DOC and UV_{254}. *J. Am. Water Works Assoc.* **2003**, *95* (3), 86-100.

11. Standard Method 1080: Reagent-Grade Water. In *Standard Methods for the Examination of Water and Wastewater,* Eaton, A. D.; Clesceri, L. S.; Greenberg, A. E., Eds.; American Public Health Association; Washington, DC, 1995; 19th ed.

12. Schaffer, R. B.; Van Hall, C. E.; McDermott, G. N.; Barth, D.; Stenger, V. A.; Sebesta, S. J.; Griggs, S. H. Application of a Carbon Analyzer in Waste Treatment. *J. Water Pollut. Control Fed.* **1965**, *37* (11), 1545-1566.

13. Van Hall, C. E.; Barth, D.; Stenger, V. A. Elimination of Carbonates from Aqueous Solutions Prior to Organic Carbon Determination. *Anal. Chem.* **1965**, *37* (6), 769-771.

14. Kaplan, L.A. Comparison of High-Temperature and Persulfate Oxidation Methods for Determination of Dissolved Organic Carbon in Freshwaters. *Limnol. Oceanogr.* **1992**, *37* (5), 1119-1125.

15. Standard Method 1050B: Significant Figures. In *Standard Methods for the Examination of Water and Wastewater,* Eaton, A. D.; Clesceri, L. S.; Greenberg, A. E., Eds.; American Public Health Association; Washington, DC, 1995; 19th ed.

16. Standard Method 5510: Aquatic Humic Substances. In *Standard Methods for the Examination of Water and Wastewater,* Eaton, A. D.; Clesceri, L. S.; Greenberg, A. E., Eds.; American Public Health Association; Washington, DC, 1995; 19th ed.

17.0 TABLES, DIAGRAMS, FLOWCHARTS, AND VALIDATION DATA

17.1 ORGANIC CARBON DETECTION LIMIT (OCDL)[a]

Dissolved Organic Carbon (DOC), mg/L					
Instrument	Fortified Conc.[b]	Mean Recovered Conc.	%RSD[c]	%REC[d]	OCDL
1	0.130	0.155	11	119	0.054
2	0.125	0.116	22	93	0.082
3	0.250	0.249	4	100	0.035
4	0.130	0.125	5	96	0.018
5	0.250	0.233	9	93	0.068
Total Organic Carbon (TOC), mg/L					
Instrument	Fortified Conc.	Mean Recovered Conc.	%RSD[c]	%REC[d]	OCDL
1	0.130	0.159	14	122	0.071
2	0.125	0.145	26	116	0.118
3	0.250	0.259	8	104	0.061
4	0.130	0.130	9	100	0.036
5	0.250	0.251	7	100	0.059

[a] Organic Carbon Detection Limits were determined by analyzing 7 replicates over 3 days.
[b] LRW fortified as specified in the table.
[c] %RSD = percent relative standard deviation
[d] %REC = percent recovery

INSTRUMENT:
1: UV/Persulfate/Wet Oxidation with Permeation/Conductivity Detection
2: Elevated Temperature/Catalyzed/Persulfate/Wet Oxidation/Nondispersive Infrared Detection (NDIR)
3: UV/Low Temperature/Persulfate/Wet Oxidation/NDIR
4: Catalyzed/Combustion Oxidation(680 °C)/NDIR
5: High Temperature Combustion Oxidation/NDIR

17.2 SINGLE TOC INSTRUMENT PRECISION AND ACCURACY

17.2.1 TOC Instrument 1: UV/persulfate wet oxidation with permeation/conductivity detection

Dissolved Organic Carbon, mg/L[a]				
Source Water	Unfortified Sample Conc.		Fortified Sample Conc.	
	Mean	%RSD	Mean	%REC
Boulder Creek	1.63	1.62	12.2	105
Shingobee R.	2.98	0.19	13.5	105
Bolten Well	1.27	0.00	12.0	107
Ohio R. (Fernbank)	2.79	0.36	13.6	108
Muddy Creek	3.81	0.15	14.6	108
Great Miami R.	3.18	0.00	13.7	104
Saint Leon Well	0.53	0.97	11.0	104
Total Organic Carbon, mg/L[a]				
Source Water	Unfortified Sample Conc.		Fortified Sample Conc.	
	Mean	%RSD	Mean	%REC
Boulder Creek	1.73	0.33	12.1	103
Shingobee R.	3.16	0.18	13.0	98
Bolten Well	1.32	0.44	11.4	100
Ohio R. (Fernbank)	3.02	0.57	13.2	102
Muddy Creek	4.24	0.00	14.6	103
Great Miami R.	3.51	0.33	13.8	102
Saint Leon Well	0.66	0.52	11.1	104

[a] N = 3, samples fortified at 10mg/L OC using KHP

17.2 SINGLE TOC INSTRUMENT PRECISION AND ACCURACY, cont'd.

17.2.2 TOC Instrument 2: Elevated temperature/catalyzed/persulfate wet oxidation/NDIR

Dissolved Organic Carbon, mg/L[a]			
Source Water	Unfortified Sample Conc.	Fortified Sample Conc.	
	Mean	Mean	%REC
Boulder Creek	1.40	11.8	104
Shingobee R.	2.58	13.3	106
Bolten Well	1.04	12.6	105
Ohio R. (Fernbank)	2.41	13.3	108
Muddy Creek	3.25	14.3	110
Great Miami R.	2.68	13.4	107
Saint Leon Well	0.40	10.6	101

Total Organic Carbon, mg/L[a]			
Source Water	Unfortified Sample Conc.	Fortified Sample Conc.	
	Mean	Mean	%REC
Boulder Creek	1.38	11.2	98
Shingobee R.	2.62	12.7	100
Bolten Well	1.05	11.4	103
Ohio R. (Fernbank)	2.46	13.1	106
Muddy Creek	3.41	13.8	104
Great Miami R.	2.89	13.2	103
Saint Leon Well	0.38	10.5	102

[a] N = 2, samples fortified at 10mg/L OC using KHP

17.2 SINGLE TOC INSTRUMENT PRECISION AND ACCURACY, cont'd.

17.2.3 TOC Instrument 3: UV/low temperature/persulfate wet oxidation/NDIR

Dissolved Organic Carbon, mg/L[a]				
Source Water	Unfortified Sample Conc.		Fortified Sample Conc.	
	Mean	%RSD	Mean	%REC
Boulder Creek	1.52	1.81	11.5	100
Shingobee R.	2.71	1.10	13.2	104
Bolten Well	1.18	1.76	11.3	101
Ohio R. (Fernbank)	2.50	0.74	13.1	106
Muddy Creek	3.38	0.81	14.0	106
Great Miami R.	2.91	0.64	13.1	102
Saint Leon Well	0.56	0.88	10.7	101

Total Organic Carbon, mg/L[a]				
Source Water	Unfortified Sample Conc.		Fortified Sample Conc.	
	Mean	%RSD	Mean	%REC
Boulder Creek	1.47	1.77	11.2	97
Shingobee R.	2.72	0.02	12.7	99
Bolten Well	1.16	2.45	11.0	98
Ohio R. (Fernbank)	2.58	1.01	12.6	100
Muddy Creek	3.18	1.28	13.5	103
Great Miami R.	2.92	1.01	13.0	101
Saint Leon Well	0.45	1.57	10.7	102

[a] N = 3, samples fortified at 10 mg/L OC using KHP

17.2 SINGLE TOC INSTRUMENT PRECISION AND ACCURACY, cont'd.

17.2.4 TOC Instrument 4: Catalyzed, 680 °C combustion oxidation/NDIR

Dissolved Organic Carbon, mg/L[a]				
Source Water	Unfortified Sample Conc.		Fortified Sample Conc.	
	Mean	%RSD	Mean	%REC
Boulder Creek	1.54	5.75	11.4	98
Shingobee R.	2.71	3.18	12.4	97
Bolten Well	1.24	1.25	12.4	98
Ohio R. (Fernbank)	2.52	5.73	12.4	98
Muddy Creek	3.56	3.17	13.3	98
Great Miami R.	3.00	6.94	12.7	96
Saint Leon Well	0.38	27.4	10.1	98

Total Organic Carbon, mg/L[a]				
Source Water	Unfortified Sample Conc.		Fortified Sample Conc.	
	Mean	%RSD	Mean	%REC
Boulder Creek	1.46	2.86	11	100
Shingobee R.	2.84	2.19	13	97
Bolten Well	1.12	1.70	11	100
Ohio R. (Fernbank)	2.81	1.79	13	100
Muddy Creek	4.04	2.02	14	96
Great Miami R.	3.42	1.66	14	101
Saint Leon Well	0.28	7.64	10	100

[a] N = 3, samples fortified at 10 mg/L OC using KHP

17.2 SINGLE TOC INSTRUMENT PRECISION AND ACCURACY, cont'd.

17.2.5 TOC Instrument 5: High temperature combustion oxidation/NDIR

Source Water	Dissolved Organic Carbon, mg/L[a]			
	Unfortified Sample Conc.		Fortified Sample Conc.	
	Mean	%RSD	Mean	%REC
Boulder Creek	1.21	1.18	11.0	98
Shingobee R.	2.29	1.15	12.0	97
Bolten Well	0.90	2.93	11.5	106
Ohio R. (Fernbank)	2.11	0.28	12.3	102
Muddy Creek	2.89	1.09	13.1	102
Great Miami R.	2.43	0.77	12.3	99
Saint Leon Well	0.38	27.4	10.0	96

Source Water	Total Organic Carbon, mg/L[a]			
	Unfortified Sample Conc.		Fortified Sample Conc.	
	Mean	%RSD	Mean	%REC
Boulder Creek	1.26	6.02	11.0	97
Shingobee R.	2.45	0.84	12.1	97
Bolten Well	0.93	1.02	10.8	98
Ohio R. (Fernbank)	2.31	1.19	12.1	98
Muddy Creek	3.34	3.40	13.1	98
Great Miami R.	2.72	0.78	12.3	96
Saint Leon Well[b]	0.32	N/A	10.0	97

[a] N = 3, samples fortified at 10 mg/L OC using KHP
[b] N = 2 for this sample, N/A = not applicable

17.3 PRECISION AND ACCURACY DATA FOR DOC AND SUVA MEASURED IN SEVEN SOURCE WATERS ON FIVE INSTRUMENTS[a]

17.3.1 DOC Measurements for Seven Source Waters, Three Replicate Instrument Injections on Five Instruments

Dissolved Organic Carbon, mg/L, Unfortified Samples								
Source Water	Inst #1	Inst #2	Inst #3	Inst #4	Inst #5	Mean	Std Dev	%RSD
Boulder Creek	1.64	1.40	1.52	1.54	1.21	1.46	0.17	11
Shingobee R.	2.98	2.58	2.71	2.71	2.29	2.66	0.25	9
Bolton Well	1.27	1.04	1.18	1.24	0.90	1.13	0.15	14
Ohio R. (Fernbank)	2.79	2.41	2.50	2.52	2.12	2.47	0.24	10
Muddy Creek	3.81	3.25	3.38	3.56	2.89	3.38	0.34	10
Great Miami R.	3.18	2.69	2.91	3.00	2.43	2.84	0.29	10
St. Leon Well	0.53	0.40	0.56	0.38	0.25	0.42	0.13	30

17.3.2 DOC Measurements for Seven Source Waters, Fortified with KHP, Three Replicate Instrument Injections on Five Instruments

Dissolved Organic Carbon, mg/L, Samples Fortified at 10 mg/L OC									
Source Water	Inst #1	Inst #2	Inst #3	Inst #4	Inst #5	Mean	Std Dev	%RSD	%REC[b]
Boulder Creek	12.2	11.8	11.5	11.4	11.0	11.6	0.43	4	101
Shingobee R.	13.5	13.3	13.2	12.4	12.0	12.9	0.62	5	102
Bolton Well	12.0	11.5	11.3	11.2	11.5	11.5	0.31	3	104
Ohio R. (Fernbank)	13.6	13.2	13.1	12.4	12.3	12.9	0.54	4	105
Muddy Creek	14.6	14.3	14.0	13.3	13.1	13.9	0.62	5	105
Great Miami R.	13.7	13.4	13.1	12.7	12.3	13.0	0.55	4	102
St. Leon Well	11.0	10.5	10.7	10.1	10.0	10.5	0.40	4	100

[a] For instrument identification (by type) see Section 6.3.
[b] % Recovery calculated as described in Section 9.8.

17.3 PRECISION AND ACCURACY DATA FOR DOC AND SUVA MEASURED IN SEVEN SOURCE WATERS ON FIVE INSTRUMENTS[a], cont'd.

17.3.3 Mean SUVA Calculation Based on the DOC Data in 17.3.1 for Seven Source Waters

Source Water	UVA (cm^{-1})	SUVA[b] (L/mg-M)					
		Inst #1	Inst #2	Inst #3	Inst #4	Inst #5	Mean
Boulder Creek	0.0432	2.62	3.08	2.84	2.97	3.58	3.02
Shingobee R.	0.0744	2.50	2.88	2.75	2.77	3.25	2.83
Bolton Well	0.0236	1.86	2.28	2.01	1.91	2.62	2.14
Ohio R. (Fernbank)	0.0727	2.60	3.01	2.90	2.88	3.43	2.97
Muddy Creek	0.1124	2.95	3.46	3.33	3.20	3.89	3.37
Great Miami R.	0.0895	2.81	3.33	3.07	3.05	3.69	3.19
St. Leon Well	0.0077	1.46	1.93	1.38	1.83	3.13	1.95

[a] For instrument identification (by type) see Section 6.3.
[b] SUVA calculated as described in Section 12.2.

17.4 PRECISION AND ACCURACY DATA FOR TOC MEASURED IN SEVEN SOURCE WATERS ON FIVE INSTRUMENTS[a]

17.4.1 TOC Measurements for Seven Source Waters, Three Replicate Instrument Injections on Five Instruments

Total Organic Carbon, mg/L, Unfortified Samples								
Source Water	Inst #1	Inst #2	Inst #3	Inst #4	Inst #5	Mean	Std Dev	%RSD
Boulder Creek	1.73	1.38	1.47	1.46	1.26	1.46	0.17	12
Shingobee R.	3.16	2.62	2.72	2.84	2.45	2.76	0.26	10
Bolton Well	1.32	1.05	1.16	1.12	0.93	1.12	0.14	13
Ohio R. (Fernbank)	3.02	2.46	2.58	2.81	2.31	2.64	0.28	11
Muddy Creek	4.24	3.41	3.18	4.04	3.34	3.64	0.47	13
Great Miami R.	3.51	2.89	2.92	3.42	2.72	3.09	0.35	11
St. Leon Well	0.66	0.39	0.45	0.28	0.32	0.42	0.15	35

17.4.2 TOC Measurements for Seven Source Waters, Fortified with KHP, from Replicate Instrument Injections on Five Instruments

Total Organic Carbon, mg/L, Samples Fortified at 10 mg/L OC									
Source Water	Inst #1	Inst #2	Inst #3	Inst #4	Inst #5	Mean	Std Dev	%RSD	%REC[b]
Boulder Creek	12.1	11.3	11.2	11.4	11.0	11.4	0.43	4	99
Shingobee R.	13.0	12.7	12.6	12.5	12.1	12.6	0.32	3	98
Bolton Well	11.4	11.4	11.0	11.2	10.8	11.1	0.28	3	100
Ohio R. (Fernbank)	13.2	13.1	12.6	12.8	12.1	12.8	0.45	4	101
Muddy Creek	14.6	13.8	13.5	13.7	13.1	13.7	0.54	4	101
Great Miami R.	13.8	13.2	13.0	13.6	12.3	13.2	0.59	5	101
St. Leon Well	11.1	10.5	10.7	10.2	10.0	10.5	0.41	4	101

[a] For instrument identification (by type) see Section 6.3.
[b] % Recovery calculated as described in Section 9.8.

17.5 INITIAL DEMONSTRATION OF CAPABILITY (IDC) REQUIREMENTS (SUMMARY)

Method Reference	Requirement	Specification and Frequency	Acceptance Criteria
Sects. 9.2.1, 9.9	Initial Demonstration of Low System Background	Analyze LRB prior to any other IDC samples.	LRBs must be ≤ 0.35 mg/L OC and ≤ 0.01 cm^{-1} UVA.
Sects. 9.2.2, 9.11	Initial Calibration Verification	After initial calibration of TOC instrument system a QCS sample is used to verify accuracy.	The analyzed value of a 1-5 mg/L calibration standard must be within $\pm 20\%$ of the true value before proceeding with the method.
Sect. 9.2.3	Initial Organic Carbon Flow Injection Memory Check	Analyze after Low System Background requirement, but before any other TOC or DOC IDC samples.	LRB injections after the highest OC-CAL injection must be ≤ 0.35 mg/L TOC.
Sect. 9.2.4	Inorganic Carbon Removal	Prior to first analysis of samples and whenever the IC removal procedure is modified.	Analysis of the IC-TEST solution after IC removal must result in a concentration of ≤ 0.35 mg/L IC, measured as OC interference.
Sect. 9.2.5	Initial Demonstration of Accuracy	Analyze 5 replicate LFBs (at 2-5 mg/L OC).	The average recovery must be $\pm 20\%$ of the true value.
Sect. 9.2.6	Initial Demonstration of Precision	Calculate precision of the accuracy samples.	The %RSD must be $\leq 20\%$.
Sect. 9.2.7	Organic Carbon Detection Limit (OCDL) Determination	Analyze 7 replicate LFBs over a period of at least 3 days at a concentration estimated to be near the DL.	The calculated OCDL must not exceed 0.35 mg/L. The mean recovery of the LFBs used in the OCDL determination must be $\pm 50\%$ of the true value.

Method Reference	Requirement	Specification and Frequency	Acceptance Criteria
Sect. 9.3.2	Initial Demonstration of Filter Membrane Suitability	Prior to the first use of filters and whenever a manufacturer or filter type is changed.	FB $\leq$ 0.35 mg/L OC and/or $\leq$ 0.01 cm^{-1} UVA. Sample filtrate OC within $\pm$ 15% of unfiltered sample OC.
Sect. 9.4.1	Initial Spectrophotometer Check	Prior to first instrument use and annually thereafter.	Test two wavelengths between 220 and 340 nm. Check manufacturer's operation manual for acceptance limits.
Sects. 9.4.2, 10.4	Spectrophotometer Performance Check	Prior to analysis of samples.	UVA within 10% of expected absorbance value.

17.6 QUALITY CONTROL REQUIREMENTS (SUMMARY)

Method Reference	Requirement	Specification and Frequency	Acceptance Criteria
Sect. 9.9	Blanks	One LRB with each TOC analysis batch. One FB with each DOC and UVA analysis batch.	TOC LRBs and DOC-FBs must be ≤ 0.35 mg/L OC. The UVA-FB must be ≤ 0.01 cm^{-1} UVA.
Sect. 8.1	Holding Time, SUVA	DOC - filtered and then acidified within 48 hours of collection. Analyzed within 28 days of time of collection.	Stored at ≤ 6 °C; preserved with acid to pH ≤ 2 after filtration.
		UVA - filtered and analyzed within 48 hours of time of collection.	Not preserved with acid, stored at ≤ 6 °C.
Sect. 8.2	Holding Time, TOC	TOC - analyze within 28 days from time of collection.	Preserved at pH ≤ 2 at the time of collection, stored at ≤ 6 °C.
Sects. 9.2, 9.3, 9.4	Initial Demonstration of Capability (IDC)	Performed whenever a new instrument is set up or when a new analyst is trained.	See Table 17.5.
Sects. 9.5, 10.3	Continuing Calibration Checks	Analysis of Low-CCC (at the MRL or below) at the beginning of each analysis batch. Subsequent CCCs analyzed after every 10 samples and after the last sample in the analysis batch, rotating concentrations to cover the calibrated range of the instrument. Mid-CCC required during each analysis batch.	Low-CCC: $\pm 50\%$ of true value. Mid-CCC: $\pm 20\%$ of true value. High-CCC: $\pm 15\%$ of true value.

Method Reference	Requirement	Specification and Frequency	Acceptance Criteria
Sect. 9.6	Field Duplicate (FD) Analyses	One FD is collected and analyzed with each analysis batch.	FD > 2 mg/L OC < 20% RPD. UVA < 10% RPD.
Sect. 9.7	Laboratory Fortified Blank (LFB) analysis	One LFB is analyzed with every DOC analysis batch.	Concentration of 1-5 mg/L OC using KHP. Recovery must be within ± 20% of true value.
Sect. 9.8	Laboratory Fortified Matrix (LFM)	One LFM is analyzed with every TOC or DOC analysis batch. Spike concentration should result in an increase in the LFM concentration of 50 to 200% of its measured or expected concentration.	Recovery outside 70-130% warrants investigation of matrix effect.
Sect. 9.11	Quality Control Sample (QCS)	The QCS is analyzed during the IDC, after each new calibration curve, each time new calibration solutions are prepared, or at least quarterly.	The analyzed value of a 1-5 mg/L QCS must be within ±20% of the true value.
Sect. 10.2	Calibration Curve	A new calibration curve is generated when fresh standards are made and/or when CCCs are out of QC limits.	Calibration curve must have $r_2 > 0.993$ before proceeding with analyses.
Sect. 10.4	Spectrophotometer performance check	The day to day performance of the spectrophotometer is checked using the COMM-SCS and/or KHP-SCS prior to analyzing any UVA sample(s).	The UVA of the KHP-SCS or COMM-SCS reading must be within 10% expected absorbance values.
Sect. 11.6.2	Spectrophotometer Blank	A second source LRW is analyzed each time spectrophotometer is zeroed.	Analysis of second source LRW must result in UVA ≤ 0.01 cm^{-1}.

FIGURE 1: FILTER BLANK PREPARATION

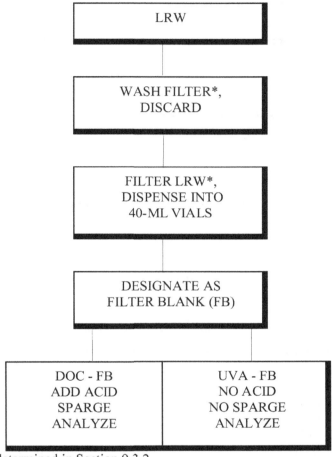

*Using volume as determined in Section 9.3.2.

FIGURE 2 : SAMPLE PREPARATION

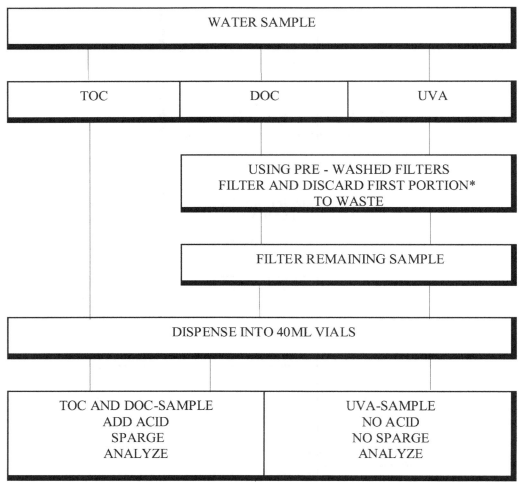

* Using volume as determined in Section 9.3.2.3.

CPSIA information can be obtained at www.ICGtesting.com
Printed in the USA
LVOW03s0100050114

368081LV00004B/335/P